THE ALTERNATIVE HOUSE

A Complete Guide to Building and Buying

By Rita Tatum

Reed Books

Los Angeles

Dedication

To M.D.M.

q
728
T

Text Copyright © 1978 by Book Developers, Inc.
Illustrations/Photographs copyright © 1978 by Book Developers, Inc.
This simultaneous Softcover and Hardcover original is published by
Reed Books, a division of Addison House, Inc. Publishing Office: Reed
Books, 9155 West Sunset Blvd., Los Angeles, California 90069.
Marketing and Sales Office: c/o Addison House, Morgan's Run,
Danbury, New Hampshire 03230.
Designed by J. C. Suarès
First edition: October 1978
ISBN 0-89169-508-7 (soft)
     0-89169-509-5 (hard)
Library of Congress Number: 78-51058
Printed in the United States of America

CONTENTS

Chapter 1
Introduction to Today's Housing Market

If you have an annual income of $20,000 or more, you can still afford the American dream. You can still buy that ivy-covered brick home in the suburbs—along with the accompanying crab-grass, dandelions and mortgage. Unfortunately, only one of every four families falls into that financial bracket.

Meanwhile, the average price for new, single-family homes is approximately $50,000. But lenders rarely make a mortgage loan for more than twice the annual income of the borrower. So, a household in the $20,000 annual income class generally can receive only a $40,000 mortgage loan. In 1976, the average family earned $14,500, while those who purchased homes brought home $21,600 a year. Of these home buyers, forty-three percent were families in which both husband and wife worked.

Industry experts—and frustrated buyers who have learned the hard way—agree that conventional home buying has gone from a mass market to a luxury market. The Joint Center for Urban Studies of the Massachusetts Institute of Technology and Harvard University reports that in 1975–76, fifty-eight percent of new homes were purchased by households with incomes higher than $20,000 a year. Another thirty-eight percent were bought by middle-income families earning between $10,000 and $20,000 annually. Only four percent of the homes bought were purchased by households with incomes totaling less than $10,000.

Only a decade earlier, the percentages were significantly different. At that time, thirty-one percent of the home buyers earned what was then considered an affluent income—more than $10,000. A full fifty-three percent were in the $5,000 to $10,000 income class. And seventeen percent were in the bottom income bracket. In a report entitled, "The Nation's Housing: 1975–1985," the joint center pointed out that forty-six percent of U.S. families could afford a new, median-priced house in 1970. But only twenty-seven percent could afford the same house in 1976. (The median price means that half the homes for sale were priced above and half below that figure.) In 1970, the median price for a new house was $23,400; by 1977, that figure had jumped to $49,000. In the early 1980s, the joint center predicts the median-priced home could be $78,000.

According to the National Association of Realtors (NAR), in November of 1977, more than forty percent of existing single-family homes were priced at $50,000 or more. Four years earlier, only fourteen percent fell into that range. Yet sales of existing single-family homes continue to hit all-time highs. NAR found that on a seasonally adjusted basis, home sales rose to 4.2 million dollars in November of 1977, a twenty-six percent increase over the $3.3 million sales total for the previous year. Even existing homes are rapidly leaving the realm of affordability for the average family. In fact, percentage increases in sales for existing homes were the highest since the NAR survey began more than ten years ago. Nationally, the median price for an existing home rose to $44,500 in November of 1977, which was 14.7 percent higher than the figure for the previous year.

Nearly half of those single-family home buyers were under age thirty-five, a trend that makes young, first-time buyers the dominant force in today's market. And nearly one-half of all buyers in the market are renters who make the transition from tenant to owner. According to the National Association of Home Builders, the pool of potential buyers is much larger than ever before. The millions of babies born following World War II are now at their prime home buying age—between twenty-five and thirty-five. They are, however, a new breed of consumers. They're weary of high costs and high taxes. They are looking for protection and relief. They recognize that housing is the best hedge they can erect against inflation. The incentive to buy is extremely strong.

Preliminary projections of nineteen-year

housing needs range between 2.1 and 2.2 million units needed annually. However, single-family housing starts for 1978 will total about 1.3 million units, with about 500,000 multi-family homes also built. Yet, even while this building is under way, 800,000 units, primarily in inner city neighborhoods, are lost each year from the nation's housing inventory through deterioration, bringing the total to less than 500,000 units annually. In other words, only one family in four will be able to buy a conventional home.

With housing prices rising an average of twelve percent a year and income increasing only eight percent, American home buyers are discovering the need for alternatives to the cottage in suburbia. Some are investing in cooperatives and condominiums, where the patch of grass is replaced by window boxes full of potted geraniums. Others are purchasing manufactured housing that they considered too ordinary three or four years ago. A few are tackling home kits such as log cabin packages, while others are investigating creative ways to save energy, such as underground living. The more adventurous are even looking into hiring an architect for a custom design, or buying a geodesic dome—two alternatives to tract housing that are no longer prohibitively expensive. Even solar energy homes are more affordable than they once were. For those who are willing to take a gamble, there's even the opportunity to buy an older home in the city and rehabilitate it. Everyone, however, seems to agree on one aspect of home buying: biding your time to save enough to buy that $67,500 ranch house in the suburbs—with an income limited to $20,000—is an exercise in futility.

The U.S. League of Savings Associations says that today's average American family saves about 5.6 percent of disposable income—personal income minus taxes. Naturally, the young family aiming for ownership saves more in an attempt to reach its goal. But even if you plan to save $1,500 a year, that is almost inconsequential as buying power for the average-priced home.

So you may have to sacrifice your dream home and buy one *now* that will help you realize the benefits of immediate ownership, such as tax deductions and enjoyment of the property. If you cannot afford your dream home of $67,500 today, what makes you think you'll have the downpayment for it by 1983? If that home increases in value at just twelve percent per year, which real estate appraisers have found accurate, that same house in 1983 will cost you an astonishing $133,200!

Many of you probably are wondering whether the "buy now" advice of the building industry is just propaganda. You may think that prices will stabilize or even come down when the frenzied pace of buying slackens. While some experts believe the annual twelve-percent inflation rate may drop somewhat in the next few years, no one is saying the cost of housing will stop going up.

In fact, some economists suggest that the housing boom of 1977 has peaked, not because of lower demand, but because of material shortages and production problems. Deliveries are taking longer. House prices are being quoted on a day-to-day basis according to the fluctuation of materials prices. During 1977, lumber prices rose twenty percent in one month, and drywall prices have risen six times in six months. Prices of asphalt for roofing now are rising at a rate three or four times greater than that of inflation. Labor also continues to increase in cost. Remember, housing suffers from inflation, not only because housing prices soar, but also because inflation makes it impossible for mortgage interest rates to go down. When rates go up, housing production is bound to go down.

As a result, it would probably take a serious, long-term downturn of the nation's economy, causing the bottom to fall out of the housing market, for price increases to slow substantially or to come down. Such a recession or depression would mean rising unemployment, declining increases in family income and lowered consumer confidence. If these statistics drop, many prospective first-time buyers will be knocked right out of the home ownership arena anyway.

In addition to all of these factors, a shortage of lots has created a market in which 1977 lot prices have risen two to four times as fast as housing prices, according to a recent U.S. Housing Markets survey. The strong, single-family market of the mid-1970s caught land developers by surprise and ran down the inventory faster than anyone expected. "In several markets, the ratio of lot value to total new-house price is hitting forty percent, compared to fifteen percent to twenty percent in the recent past," the researchers noted.

The survey painted the bleakest picture for housing lots in Baltimore, Maryland; Washington, D.C.; Florida's Miami-Fort Lauderdale area; Denver, Colorado; California's Los Angeles and Orange County, as well as San Diego and the San Francisco-Oakland area. In these areas, lot shortages are so severe that they will curtail housing starts for several years to come.

In most of the surveyed markets, prices of finished lots increased an average of thirty percent during 1977. In some cases, that increase has even reached fifty percent. The survey reported that the minimum price of a subdivision lot in a stable, white-collar area is now $20,000 in half the major housing markets.

In California, the lot price represented thirteen to fifteen percent of the total home price in 1976. In 1978, it accounts for forty percent of the new-house price, and for thirty to thirty-five percent in many sections of Baltimore, Washington, D.C., and Florida's Dade County (the Miami area).

"To find cheaper land, it is necessary to go sixty-five miles out of the city center in New York-Long Island, forty-five to fifty miles out in Los Angeles, forty miles out in Philadelphia, the Washington area and San Francisco," the report said.

Outside the South, lot development prices have increased an average of about twenty percent since the 1972–73 housing boom. They've doubled in San Francisco and Seattle, Washington. In addition, inspection and tap-in fees are rising steadily, sometimes in $2,000 to $4,000 increments, as in Washington's neighboring Fairfax (Virginia) County and Baltimore's neighboring Harford County.

To combat these lot shortages, condominiums and cooperatives are enjoying a sales upsurge. In 1977, condominium production totaled 200,000 units, with an additional 100,000 units converted from apartment buildings into condominiums. More than one-third of the condominiums built in 1977 were erected in California, where lots for home building are restricted. The largest number of conversions—and particularly strong markets for new condominium buildings—were found in Chicago; Houston, Texas; California's San Diego and Los Angeles; and Washington, D.C.

The condominium boom comes in part from the changing lifestyle of many Americans. The young home buyer, often single or married but childless, prefers to be in the core of the city, close to the office and the cultural and entertainment opportunities offered by the urban centers. With energy costs increasing, long commutes from the suburbs are becoming less practical. These citizens, however, are tired of renting. They desire the investment advantage of ownership, but they don't want the typical builder/developer type of house that spells sterility and monotony to them. They prefer the originality offered by many older structures. They welcome the opportunity to create their own living environment by rehabilitating older inner-city dwellings.

Because the costs of energy can make up a major portion of their monthly expenses—at least during the winter—a number of homeowners are choosing solar energy homes. A few years ago, a solar collector system for private homes was out of the reach of many buyers. Today, however, some systems can be incorporated into prefabricated, manufactured housing systems that compete with their conventionally-built neighbors in cost.

The really energy-conscious home buyer also is curious about the latest in experimental living—underground housing. Our forefathers emerged from the caves generations ago; a number of Americans are showing interest in returning to their roots in order to save on heating and cooling costs. Underground housing is truly energy efficient, because the earth acts as a natural insulator.

Dome homes, made popular by the 1960s counterculture, also are gaining respectability with families who are concerned about energy costs. Since the dome's shell is smaller in area than a conventional home with the same square footage, dome dwellers can save on their heating and cooling bills. In addition, the shape of the home is quite distinctive. The price is at least competitive with more conventional new housing and, in some cases, it can even be less expensive.

Log cabins also can cost less than conventional homes. They offer a distinctively warm atmosphere that cannot be duplicated in a ranch or split-level home. They also offer a "personality" that conventional housing often cannot.

Factory-built housing provides the owner with a home that he or she may not otherwise be able to afford. Frequently the home doesn't look at all like its predecessor, the mobile home trailer. For people who can afford only $20,000 to $35,000 for a home, this is an excellent alternative to conventional housing. The homes are well designed and feature all the modern amenities found in traditional housing, plus some.

Another reason home buyers are looking into alternative housing is the increasing number of singles interested in the investment advantages of owning rather than renting. Lenders say that purchases by single people are increasing because more individuals are choosing not to marry, but are seeking the equity and tax advantages that home ownership provides.

Statistics show that young people now fre-quently marry at twenty-five years or older. Many single people have well-paying jobs. They tire of renting and wish to buy a place of their own. The enactment of the Equal Opportunity Act in 1975, which prohibits discrimination on the basis of sex or marital status in granting mortgage loans, has helped a number of single people, especially women, obtain home loans. The law also requires lenders to consider alimony and child support as income, allowing more women to become home buyers.

In the past, lenders often looked on single or divorced women as poor credit risks. However, they are now discovering that they were excluding a significant portion of the mortgage loan market. In addition, women can now establish credit in their own names rather than in their husbands' names. Widowed or divorced women are no longer robbed of their financial identity.

There is also an upsurge in singles who buy homes together. In many cases, these individuals share living quarters with unrelated people of the opposite sex. The number of these shared households nearly doubled between 1970 and 1976. Currently, about 1.5 million people are sharing households.

The number of singles—especially young singles—who want to own their own piece of property is definitely a significant portion of the home buying market. A study at Princeton University showed a marked increase in the number of single home buyers since 1970. That trend is expected to continue. The Princeton study predicts that thirty percent of the people thirty years old and single will buy homes.

All of these factors have led to exciting new alternatives in the housing market. Some of them are documented in this book; others, even more creative, are bound to develop as Americans look for ways to own a home that the current housing industry cannot supply.

Chapter 2

Buying a House You Can Afford

If you're just beginning to shop for your first home, you may have heard that you should be looking at a house that costs two and a half times your gross annual income. In other words, if you are making $20,000 a year, you may think you can afford a $50,000 home. But if you check with your friendly neighborhood banker, you will find that he or she uses completely different parameters.

Before you start looking seriously for a home, consult your personal banker and several of the mortgage lenders close to your proposed home-site. Based on your income and several other factors, they will tell you how much they will lend you.

Although it may appear that lenders draw the magic figures for mortgages out of little black books they keep in their desks, you can actually estimate what you're worth to a lender rather simply. Today, most mortgage lenders calculate how much you can afford to borrow for your home in terms of your monthly cash flow. Legally, the lender must consider all steady income of both the husband and wife, as well as part-time income, alimony and child support, if these items are steady income.

Before the lender quotes the terms to you, he or she also will carefully analyze any long-term debts you may have, such as car payments and revolving charge accounts. Essentially, any debt that extends beyond seven months is considered a long-term loan, and will be included in the lender's evaluation. Consequently, if you owe only twelve months of payments on your car, you may wish to pay a few months ahead, so it will be regarded as a short-term loan.

After the lender has determined all of your long-term debt obligations, he or she will review your job stability, financial history and credit record to see how well you pay your debts. The lender also will check to see if you have enough money set aside to meet the downpayment and closing costs—charges that are paid when you sign your mortgage loan. The closing costs include the lender's fee for processing the loan and other expenses.

From your personal financial data, the lender determines approximately how much you will be able to borrow—and pay back. Generally, lenders insist that your monthly payments for principal, interest, taxes and insurance total no more than twenty-five to thirty percent of your gross monthly income. In addition, all of your other long-term debts, including the mortgage, should not exceed thirty-five percent of your gross monthly income.

After the lender determines your monthly housing allowance, he or she will refer to a mortgage schedule, which shows monthly principal and interest payments for various types of loans. When you actually apply for a loan, the lender also will consider the market conditions and other housing expenses such as taxes, insurance and utilities.

When planning to buy a home, you must consider not only the downpayment, but also the closing costs and fees for lawyers, appraisers and home inspectors' professional counsel. You'll have to set aside enough money to cover moving expenses, as well as for purchasing appliances and furniture and for payment of utility, maintenance and repair bills.

Before you agree to use any particular form of financing for your home, shop around carefully. Become familiar with the various types of home loans that may be available to you.

Conventional Loans
Made by private lending institutions, conventional loans comprise eighty percent of all money lent for mortgages. They are made to anyone the lender considers a good credit risk. To receive a conventional loan, you probably will have to wait only a few days. You borrow as much as the lender thinks you can afford to pay back over a negotiated period of time. Frequently the repayment period for a conventional loan is shorter than for loans backed by either the Federal Housing Authority or the Veterans Administration.

For conventional loans, both downpayments and interest rates are higher than FHA- or VA-backed loans. The common downpayment is twenty to twenty-five percent of the house's appraised value. However, with the increased cost of housing and the availability of mortgage insurance, some lenders write loans with as little as five to ten percent down. Paid either as part of your closing costs or as a portion of your monthly payment, private mortgage insurance protects the lender's risk.

FHA-insured Loans

For the first-time buyer, FHA insures mortgages against default on both new and existing houses. Basically, FHA is designed to encourage lenders to provide financing for home buyers with limited incomes. One advantage of the FHA-backed loan is a low downpayment. Currently, the downpayment is three percent of the first $25,000 of the FHA-appraised value and five percent of the remainder, up to $60,000. Repayment periods also are longer than conventional loans, frequently extending thirty to thirty-five years. Some are even granted on forty-year repayment periods. Interest rates are fixed by FHA, but the buyer does pay an additional half percent for the FHA mortgage insurance premium.

Besides conventional housing, mobile home purchases also benefit from the FHA plan. For a single-width unit, you can borrow a maximum of $15,000. However, you should know that many lenders balk at FHA-backed loans because of the red-tape, paperwork and time involved. So mortgage banking companies write many of the FHA-insured loans.

Nevertheless, anyone can apply for an FHA-insured loan at an FHA-approved lending institution. After applying, you will have to wait while the application is sent to the local FHA office. Required to meet certain minimum, government-set standards, the house will then be appraised by the FHA. After reviewing the appraisal, the FHA will determine what amount will be insured. If the FHA determines the applicant will be able to make the payments—and the lender agrees—the loan is granted.

You may be somewhat confused about the term "points," also referred to as "discount points." These will be encountered by anyone buying a home with either an FHA-insured or a VA-guaranteed loan. Since the interest rates on these loans are fixed, and often lower than conventional loans, the lender must make up the difference to insure that a profit is made on the loan. To compensate for the difference in interest rates between government-supported loans and conventional loans, the lender assesses additional charges, or points.

Basically, one point is equal to one percent of the mortgage loan. With FHA-insured or VA-guaranteed loans, the seller is required to pay the points at the closing. However, you will end up paying for these points, because the smart seller will add them to the asking price of the home.

Sometimes the lender also charges points to the buyer. If your state has an interest ceiling (limiting the amount of interest a lender can charge), the lender might charge points to raise the income from the loan up to the market rates. Without those points, the lender couldn't afford to write home loans. The points can, however, vary from one lending institution to another. If you know that lenders in your area use points, you should shop around for financing. You also may be able to negotiate with the seller to split the cost of the points between both of you. In that case, make sure the arrangement is written into your offer to buy the home.

VA-guaranteed Loans

Since the end of World War II, the Veterans Administration (VA) has supported loans for eligible veterans who wish to buy either new or used homes. The VA guarantees up to sixty percent or $17,500 (whichever is lower) of a loan made to buy or build a home. Like FHA-backed loans, VA-guaranteed loans require an appraisal of the property. However, there is no limit on the amount of money that may be borrowed. If you qualify, you can borrow one hundred percent of the appraised value, as long as the mortgage doesn't exceed the appraised value and the lender doesn't require a downpayment.

Interest rates also are favorable, and repayment periods are often twenty-five to thirty years. Most veterans are eligible for this loan, as are the husbands or wives of soldiers who died while in the service or from a disability incurred in the service. Even veterans who have used the loan program before and paid it back can qualify for another VA-guaranteed loan.

For additional information, consult your local VA office, or write the Veterans Administration, Washington, D.C. 20420.

FmHA Loans
For rural-area buyers with limited incomes, the Farmers Home Administration (FmHA) offers loans. To be eligible for this loan, you must prove that you cannot obtain a conventional loan, and you must buy a home in a community with a population of 20,000 or less, outside a standard metropolitan area. Essentially, the FmHA program is divided into two categories of home buyers. One is for families or single people with less than $10,000 in annual income. These individuals may qualify for interest credits that can reduce the interest rate to as little as one percent. The other area of FmHA loans is for persons or families with incomes greater than $10,000 but less than $15,600—for which they pay eight percent interest on home loans.

The FmHA will loan one hundred percent of the appraised value of the house, so a downpayment isn't required. However, most homes financed by FmHA are in the $25,000 to $35,000 range and the maximum loan period is thirty-three years. Once the loan is granted, the FmHA annually reviews the borrower's income. When the borrower's income reaches the point at which he or she qualifies for conventional financing, the FmHA requires the borrower to obtain such a loan.

Additional information on FmHA loans can be obtained from any local FmHA or FHA office. You can also write to the Farmers Home Administration, U.S. Department of Agriculture, Washington, D.C. 20250.

Other Loans
Recently, lenders have been testing alternatives to conventional mortgages. These forms are often designed for the individual's financial status, making them easier to obtain for first-time buyers. They often do not rely on the conventional mortgage's fixed interest rate, fixed terms and fixed payments.

Some of the loan instruments covered here are not permitted where federal or state regulations restrict the payment of interest on interest or prohibit escalating mortgage payments. However, Congress is considering laws that would relax some of the restrictions. The Federal Home Loan Bank Board, which regulates federally chartered savings and loans as well as loan associations, may also make recommendations to promote use of more creative mortgaging.

One of these newer loan programs is the *Variable Rate Mortgage*, popular in California. Not offered everywhere, the variable rate mortgage is gaining popularity because the interest rate fluctuates, usually connected to the lender's cost of obtaining loan funds. This mortgage allows lenders hurt by tight money and high inflation to stay in the home mortgage market. It can be a good plan for buyers who plan to sell their homes in the near future. In addition, many variable rate mortgages do not carry prepayment penalties.

The *Graduated Payment Mortgage* is designed for young, first-time buyers—often those who have limited incomes. Basically, this mortgage features initially low monthly payments that increase over a five- to ten-year period, depending on the payment plan. Naturally, these payments start out lower than the more conventional loans and become higher than a fixed payment rate later. Lenders who offer this program assume that the borrower's income will increase. It allows young home buyers to qualify for a loan with less income than they would need under a conventional loan. However, the buyer probably will build little or no equity during the early stages of repayment.

For those with good potential incomes, the *Flexible Payment Mortgage* allows the borrower to pay only the interest during the loan's first five years, permitting some people to qualify sooner for home loans. At the end of those five years, the owner begins payment on the actual money borrowed and payments are increased at a rate that will retire the loan balance by the end of the loan's term.

The *Deferred Interest Mortgage* permits the borrower to begin the payments with a lower interest rate. Under this mortgage, all of the interest and any additional fee for this type of loan is paid either later in the mortgage payments or when the house is sold to another person.

The *Flexible Loan Insurance Program Mortgage* also assumes the borrower's income will increase. In this program, you put part of the downpayment into a pledged savings account. Then to supplement the monthly payments, which are reduced for the first five years, a portion is withdrawn from the savings account. Naturally, this program requires higher interest rates over the life of the loan. But it does help you if you don't have the initial income to qualify for a more conventional loan.

For older people on fixed incomes, the *Reverse Annuity Mortgage* allows the buyer to use the home's equity. Regular payments to the homeowner are made under this program by the lender. When the estate is settled, after the owner's death or when the property is sold to another homeowner, the lender collects the debt.

Regardless of the financing you choose, make sure you check thoroughly on the lending institution. Currently, no public office keeps close tabs on mortgage bankers. You will do well to shop carefully for an institution that is known for its sound business practices and reputable dealings with customers.

Chapter 3
Bringing in the Professionals

Uninitiated home buyers often spurn architects because they fear their hard-earned money will be used as a financial outlet for the architect's desires. In fact, many people still look forward to working with an architect about as much as they enjoy discussing a root canal in a back molar with a dentist. However, most architects are not that intimidating, nor are their home designs necessarily so far out that you would feel you were "living in a glass house." Every house in this country, no matter how common in appearance, was designed by someone.

While a good architect certainly has no desire to ignore esthetics, he or she can channel creativity to meet your needs. The late, great architect Louis Kahn once said that he didn't want clients who knew precisely what they wanted, down to every window and dormer. He preferred working for clients "who knew what they aspired to."

The ideal client for most architects has a highly developed sense of taste and is eager for quality as well as individuality. At the same time, however, the ideal client lacks the solution. Otherwise, there's really no need for an architect, only someone to execute the design, such as a general contractor.

If you fit this description, all you need to remember to promote a good architect-client relationship is that the architect is working for you, not the other way around. If you don't like the designs of one architect, look for another one who is doing designs you do like.

Finding an architect is like finding a family doctor. You'll probably want to begin your search by talking to friends and acquaintances who have recently built homes. Many owners will be quite willing to discuss the experience they had with their architect. If you are new in town, you may have to use a slightly different route in your initial search.

Professional ethics forbid the American Institute of Architects (AIA) from recommending architects. However, the local chapters of the AIA generally have current files of their members' work that you may make an appointment to see. (For a list of AIA local chapters, see page 148.) When you find two or three styles you like, you can then follow up by making an appointment and talking with each architect personally.

In addition to the AIA, you may wish to contact the American Institue of Building Designers (AIBD). There is one major difference between AIA and AIBD: architects are licensed by the state. Those who use AIA after their names have passed examinations given by the association, and have agreed to abide by the AIA code of ethics. While building designers have some architectural training, most states do not require them to obtain licenses. If you are considering using a building designer, keep this distinction in mind.

Architectural services are not cheap. But remember that you're hiring a person to design what is probably the largest single investment you will make in your lifetime—your home.

The architect's fee depends on the cost of the job and the amount of design, construction supervision and other work involved. These expenses can be figured by the architect in a number of ways, depending on the job. For some jobs, the architect bases his or her fee on a percentage of the total building costs, often ten to fifteen percent of the total package price for full architectural services. Architects also can be paid on an hourly or daily rate, may choose to charge you a multiple of their direct expenses or work for a flat fee.

A tight budget shouldn't necessarily prevent you from hiring an architect. In fact, if your finances are limited, you may be wise to see an architect, because he or she will be able to expose you to a wide range of options that can make your home esthetic and functional for less expense than you thought possible.

When you pay $250 for a three-piece suit, you know it's worth your while to pay an additional $25 to have it tailored. You know that the suit was mass-produced to fit some ideal model that

no living individual seems to duplicate. Why shouldn't you at least consider hiring an architect, instead of purchasing a house constructed from stock blueprints?

Many times an architect's expertise can save you money, thus expanding your range of home options. That knowledge can be tapped to assist you. For instance, an architect can help you choose an alternative in siding that is just as appealing as the one you wanted, but cheaper and stronger structurally.

If you have chosen to buy stock plans from a contractor, he or she may object to making substitutions or modifications, but an architect can offer options that often will not require making major structural changes or modifications that push up your costs. A good architect frequently can design a house at a cost very close to what you might pay a contractor for a set of plans that came straight from a file cabinet.

Naturally, finding the right architect isn't easy. You have to be willing to shop around, querying friends and acquaintances who have recently used architectural services in building their homes. You should try to visit recent architectural work in your area to see what kind of styles appeal to your personal taste. If you like everything squared off, you should stay away from an architect obsessed with curves and circles. On the other hand, if you absolutely abhor boxy structures, finding them both confining and too ordinary for your preferences, that same architect may be the one for you.

In addition to well established architects, who tend to be more expensive, you may wish to consider hiring architectural students who are about to graduate from a good, local architectural school. Recent graduates make good sources for the client with high design aspirations and financial resources suited to the "Early Poverty" orange crate school of design. Many of these designers begin their careers by working out of their homes rather than offices. They will provide designs for additions, remodeling jobs and

homes. Since these recent graduates have little overhead, this saving will be indirectly passed on to you in reduced fees.

Like other professional associations, most architectural schools will not recommend one architectural student over another. Most schools, however, will provide you with a list of advanced students or recent graduates willing to take on projects.

After you have initially narrowed down your choice of architects to three or four, make an appointment with each. During the appointments, you will be able to ask questions and see additional work by the architects. You might be attracted to this one's work, but that one's attitude. Don't be flustered. Once you have shopped around, you'll find one architect with whom you have a good rapport, which is essential to your home's completion. In addition, you should talk to the architect's former clients, asking them about their experiences.

When you sit down with an architect, be prepared to discuss your needs. Both your present and future needs should be outlined, as well as your lifestyle. The more the architect knows about you, your family and your personal tastes; the easier it will be for him to design a home that you will fall in love with.

In working with an architect, you must provide him or her with complete information concerning the building site. If you haven't bought a lot or if you are having trouble finding the kind of lot you want, most architects will be happy to help you in the lot selection. Once the site is bought, the architect will study the topography, soil conditions, orientation of the home on the site and many other physical features to help the designer develop a home that suits both you and the site.

You should tell the architect what you can afford to pay for the total house package, including the lot, the house and the design services. Outline your budget to the architect, so that he can help you evaluate what can be done within

Designed by architect Stanley
Tigerman, A.I.A., this house
is located on a 2½ acre plot of
land.

Located in a Chicago suburb,
this house was designed by
Stanley Tigerman, A.I.A.

Above and facing page:
This weekend vacation house was designed for a couple who live in Chicago, and was named "The Hot Dog House" because it is long and narrow. Designed by architect Stanley Tigerman, A.I.A., the house features an opaque wood wall on one side, and windows on the other.

your budget's limitations.

Although a few architects prepare sketches of floor plans and elevations with rough dimensions and then let you take these to a drafting service, most will not recommend this approach, because they believe they aren't properly servicing their client.

Whatever you do, make sure that you know exactly what the architect will do for the stated fee. Besides the items outlined earlier, the fee is based partially on the extent of the architect's involvement. For instance, you may wish the architect to act as a project supervisor. In this role, the architect will check on the building's progress, verify the correct use of materials, and maintain records of the contractor payments and all of the guarantees on completion of your home.

Generally, the architect interprets the client's needs and correlates those needs to the given budget. The architect also studies the site in detail and draws preliminary sketches, including the floor plans and the general exterior appearance. The architect also frequently prepares preliminary cost estimates.

If you still want to make changes, make them before the architect begins the final working drawings and details—blueprints that will show the contractor how to construct your home. Once construction has begun, any design changes you decide to make will be very expensive.

After the architect has your approval, he or she will prepare the specifications, a detailed listing of all the materials and methods to be used in the project. Architects also prepare information for the contracts that will govern the general contractor's, and sometimes the subcontractor's, work. The architect also will advise you on the selection of a contractor if you haven't already picked one out. He or she may suggest you hire a contractor through competitive bidding to get the best price. In competitive bidding, a number of contractors provide the architect with their bids for the job. The architect reviews each proposal and recommends the best contractor for the job

to the client.

If you wish, the architect can also inspect the construction progress for you and work directly with the contractor on any last-minute changes in the original plan. He or she can also handle contractor payments and inspect the finished product prior to your move-in date.

In further efforts to keep costs down, some architects combine design with actual construction. "Design/build" firms, as they are frequently called, agree to produce a complete house for a client, similar to the services of a contractor. However, they offer custom designs, rather than standard plans, as part of the package.

Most design/build firms begin their initial contact with the client as any architect would. They discuss with you design requirements, personal tastes and financial limitations. Then the firm provides a preliminary design. If you approve the design, working drawings are prepared, just as in a more conventional architectural firm.

Generally, you sign a contract for the complete price of the house. You should check to see who picks up the tab, however, if the cost is higher than the initial estimate. Some firms are organized to absorb the difference, while others require the client to assume these expenses.

With the possible exception of buying a condominium, any home alternative you opt for that is covered in this book will require the services of a building contractor or builder. Choose a reputable firm, known for constructing solid houses.

Often, you will hear the terms "contractor" and "builder" used interchangeably. However, they are different. A general or building contractor enters into a contract with you to do work. The contractor is completely responsible for the total construction of your home. Whether you're building a custom house designed by an architect or one ordered from a mail-order company, you're going to work with a general contractor.

The contractor is responsible for the workmen on the project. He or she has to make sure all the necessary people are on the job at the specified

time. For instance, the plumber should not be scheduled to arrive two weeks before the site excavation is completed. The general contractor also arranges for all the subcontractors who will be doing the excavating, framing, plumbing, wiring and installing of the heating and cooling systems. The contractor must make sure that the specified materials are used in the specified manner.

Unlike a contractor, a builder does not work as your agent. Frequently, the builder constructs speculative houses and offers them for sale to any buyer. So if you're buying a manufactured house (covered in more detail in Chapter 11), you'll probably work with a builder. A builder offers you the services of construction in return for your purchase of his or her product.

If you are using an architect, he or she may recommend several competent contractors to build your home. If you are not using an architect, you should get references from friends who have used contractors. You also can research local builders through your local chapter of the National Association of Home Builders and the Better Business Bureau. The Better Business Bureau will tell you if any complaints have been filed against the contracting firm.

Before you sign a contract, find out about warranties the builder or contractor offers on the house's construction. While many contractors and builders provide one-year warranties, the Home Owners Warranty (HOW) provides a ten-year protection plan for new houses. Developed by the NAHB, the program is probably the best coverage you can find. However, it is only offered by member-builders of NAHB. (For a list of the local chapters of NAHB, see page 149.)

You need a warranty to protect you in case you discover major structural or mechanical defects a month after you move into the home. Recognizing that consumers often don't check this aspect thoroughly, a number of states have enacted implied warranty laws that make the seller liable for defects in materials or workman-

ship. But implied warranties cannot really replace written ones in a court of law. In fact, the federal government requires builders and marketers of new homes with Federal Housing Authority mortgage insurance to provide written warranties.

HOW provides a one-year warranty against defects in materials and workmanship, a two-year warranty for defects in major mechanical systems and a ten-year warranty for major structural defects. To participate in HOW, builders must meet NAHB's standards of technical competence, financial soundness and reputable dealing with customers. Builders who belong to the HOW program also agree to build according to HOW's standards.

During the second year of the HOW warranty, the customer is protected against defects in the wiring, plumbing, heating and cooling systems. For the first two years, American Bankers Insurance Company of Florida, which underwrites the HOW program, backs the builder's written guarantee. If the builder folds or won't pay his warranty obligations, American Bankers assumes that responsibility.

For the final eight years of HOW a national insurance plan underwritten by American Bankers directly insures the home you buy against major structural defects. Using HOW's definition, a major structural defect is actual damage to the load-bearing portion of the home, including damage done because the house has settled or expanded due to lateral soil movement.

An additional plus that HOW offers is its system for settling disagreements. HOW is designed to keep disputes out of the courts, which holds down costs for both builder and buyer. Generally, problems can be resolved between the builder and the buyer. However, if you cannot solve the problem within the first two years, you can contact the local HOW council. Licensed to operate as wholly owned subsidiaries of their respective home builders associations, these local or state councils can be contacted for help during the first two years of the HOW program. There are about one hundred councils throughout the country.

The council will attempt to help the buyer and the builder reach an agreement that is acceptable to both parties. If that fails, the buyer can request conciliation. Then the local HOW council appoints a neutral mediator to investigate the problem and clarify the issue so the parties can agree. As a final resort, the homeowner can request non-binding arbitration, which is arranged through the American Arbitration Association through the local HOW council.

For the final eight years of the HOW program, the buyer can make claims for defects directly to the local council or to a representative of the insurance company. If either the buyer or the insurer is unsatisfied with the finding on the claim, arbitration can be requested.

Unfortunately, even though the HOW program is currently offered by approximately 6,000 builders in forty-four states, it is not available to all home buyers. The drawback to the program is that HOW is voluntary. It is limited to participating builders where the local home builders association permits HOW to operate. Customers of builders who operate where the program isn't available are not protected. Until there's a homeowner's protection warranty available at the buyer's option, you may be better protected if you choose a builder who offers HOW.

Although the builder pays for the HOW coverage, this cost is passed on to you, the buyer. However, the cost of HOW coverage is only $2 per thousand of the home's selling price. So a house that costs $60,000 would have an additional cost of $120 to pay for the HOW program. When you consider the possible alternatives, including lawyers' fees to fight the builder in court for three or four years, that $120 is a definite bargain.

If you plan to hire a contractor, you should get bids from at least four firms. Your architect can help you decide which is the best bid. The architect will supply each contractor with identical plans and specifications. The designer will also alert each contractor that you are getting bids from other firms. He or she will give each firm a date, often three or four weeks from the day the contractor is supplied with the plans and specifications, when the bids will be reviewed.

If you have an architect, he or she will help you review each of the bids. If you are not using an architect, you may wish to seek the advice of your lending institution. Either the architect or the lender may advise you to accept a bid that is not the lowest you receive. Since both professionals are experienced in building, you should be guided by their reasoning. The lowest bidder may wish to make substitutions that are not in your best interest. The lowest bid does spell the best short-range economy, but it doesn't necessarily imply the best long-term economy and quality.

After you have arranged for both long-term financing and a short-term construction loan, you are ready to sign a contract with the contractor or builder. As you enter the final negotiation phase, make sure that everything is outlined in writing.

If you are purchasing a custom or mail-order plan house, make sure that your final payment isn't due until you receive an affidavit from the contractor or builder certifying that all material suppliers, laborers and subcontractors are paid. This will prevent you from having any subcontractors' liens placed on your house.

The contractor should also agree to maintain certain types of insurance coverage, including workmen's compensation policies. When the work is finished, the contractor should include provisions in his contract for a complete clean-up of the premises. If you have an architect, he or she will make sure that all the materials specified by brand name and model number are the ones you have in your home. If you don't have an architect, be sure the builder or contractor includes a provision in the contract that will not allow substitutions without your consent.

Bringing in the Professionals

Reputable contractors guarantee their work for at least one year. If anything goes wrong within that time period, the contractor will repair defects. But you should make sure that this paragraph is in the contract you sign.

The contractor is also required to secure all the necessary building permits, unless his contract exempts him from this responsibility. Check to see who is handling the permits. Sometimes your architect may be overseeing the building code permits. The contractor will date and initial all plans and specifications and should be allowed to make changes *only* with your mutual consent. If you are planning to do any of the finishing work yourself, you should make sure that this portion is specifically excluded from the contracted work.

The general contractor usually receives cash payments in installments, based on satisfactory completion of each phase of the work. Check with your architect to see how much is paid for each section of the work. Frequently, ten percent of the installment is withheld until you give your final approval of the job.

A local authority on building and zoning should review both your contract and the house plans before you sign the contract. You should also have your attorney review the contract before you place your signature on the dotted line.

If you are buying a builder house, you will sign a contract to buy the finished home. This contract should carry at least a one-year warranty on the house and the workmanship in its construction.

As soon as the first shovel digs into the ground, you should begin keeping records of all payments made. You may have your architect check the contractor's records for materials, equipment, appliances, labor and subcontractor payments. As you make each payment to the contractor, you may wish to request copies of partial lien waivers from subcontractors. These waivers indicate that the subcontractors have been partially paid for their services and supplies. When you make the final payment to the contractor, make sure you receive copies of all the subcontractors' final lien waivers, which indicate that you and your local bank now own the building completely.

As with any other form of contract, your final responsibility ends when the project is completed. Check to verify that all of the payments are being used for work that has been performed, or for materials, equipment and appliances that meet the specifications of the contract.

Situating your home on its lot and arranging the floor plan to suit your family's needs are two of the most important points in arriving at your dream house. Again, an architect can be indispensable in guiding you through these steps. The following details should help you work effectively with your architect on these personal touches.

Siting the Home

If you are hiring an architect, he or she may discuss your home's siting with you. Architects often divide the lot into public, service and private areas. Essentially, the public area consists of the front lawn. The service area encompasses the driveway, sidewalks, washer and dryer and trash disposal sections of the lot. The rest of the lot, including the back yard, is considered private area.

To reduce the public area and increase the privacy of your home, architects will often recommend that your home be set forward on the lot with small spaces to the sides. That gives you more back yard space, and therefore more private space.

Frequently, the architect will tuck service areas into the side of the house, near the garage. If your lot is right on top of your neighbors, the architect might also recommend that one side of your house, where the bedrooms are located, have either reduced windows or none at all. This allows you more privacy. The living spaces should look out on the most attractive parts of your landscape.

Checking Floor Plans

The floor plan shown on the preceding page is a typical example, whether you're using an architect or buying a condominium or modular home. Actually, coming up with a good floor plan is not as complex as it might seem. You should, however, pay particular attention to the plans, because the overall layout of the home will affect you every day.

Like the lot, the floor plan can be divided into what architects sometimes refer to as zones. Every home has three zones—working, living and sleeping. Most often, the working zone includes the garage, workroom, kitchen, main entry and hallway. The living zone includes the dining room and the living room, while the sleeping zone covers bathrooms adjacent to the bedrooms and the bedrooms themselves.

Generally, you will want the work rooms and the sleeping rooms separated in some manner. In this plan, they are separated by the living room. Although you may want the washer and dryer near the bedrooms, you need to remember that this area will be noisy.

In addition, a well designed house has built-in buffer zones. Buffer zones help deaden noise and add privacy to bedrooms. Buffer zones generally are closets that will hold linens or clothes to help deaden sound waves passing from a noisy area, such as the main hallway, into a quieter bedroom. Bookshelves or storage units also can act as buffer zones, as can carpeted stairways.

Even if the house you like doesn't already have buffer zones where you want them, you often can add these yourself. You may, for instance, want a set of bookcases on the wall next to the master bedroom to keep the noise of living room parties from disturbing sleepers.

Traffic patterns also play a key role in a well-designed house. You usually need one main entrance to receive company, but you'll also want a second entrance that is designed a little more ruggedly, so that your son's dirty sneakers don't track creatures from the black lagoon into your living room as soon as he enters the house. If the second entrance is located near kitchen and workroom areas which are tiled, you may be able to catch him before he strolls onto the white living room rug. If you don't catch him, at least some of the dirt will be left on the tile anyway.

You should set up the traffic patterns that are typical of your family. Many couples find a garage located near the kitchen makes the trips from the car to the refrigerator with groceries much easier.

Hallways do a terrific job of handling traffic. However, they also are frequently used for nothing else. Therefore, many homes have little or no hallway space. Bedrooms should dead end: that is, you shouldn't be able to trek through one to get to another. It's also nice if the living room dead ends, too. That way, your flu-ridden husband doesn't have to traipse through your evening club meeting to help himself to some grapefruit juice in the kitchen.

When you're looking at the kitchen area, imagine that you have to travel through with the doors to the refrigerator, oven and dishwasher wide open. If you can open all simultaneously and move effectively around them, the kitchen's layout may not be troublesome. However, if you imagine opening the kitchen door, only to realize that you have just dented both it and the already open oven door, you'll have problems working in the kitchen.

If you have a considerable collection of furniture, you'll want to arrange it mentally within the house's parameters. One way to see how everything will fit is to measure your furniture and then cut out small pieces of paper that are scaled to the floor plan. Like road maps, floor plans nearly always have the scale dimensions in the lower right-hand corner. If you find out that you have a 102-inch wall right where you wanted to place a 104-inch sofa that you'll never part with, you may wish to consider rearranging either the sofa or the floor plan you're using.

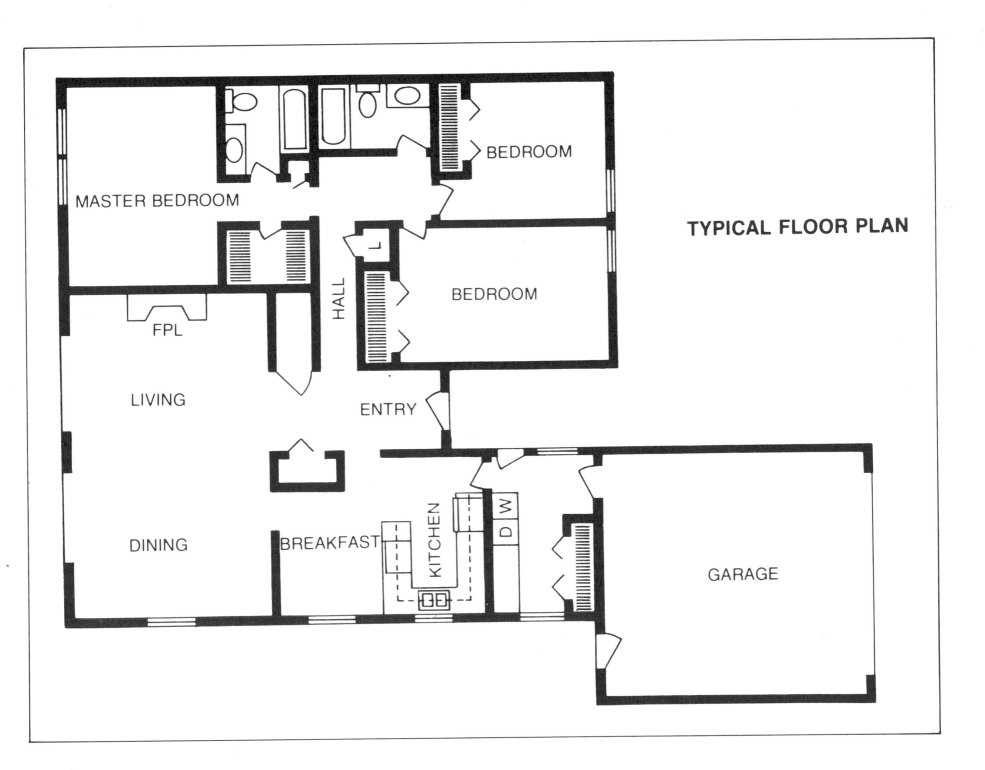

Chapter 4

Making Your House Snug

The continual rise in oil prices and the resulting increase in electricity rates are, in effect, decreasing the amount of spendable income you have. In addition, experts predict that future homeowners will receive certain tax breaks for modifications they make on their homes that help the nation cut back its massive energy usage. Nevertheless, many homeowners still are not convinced that energy saving devices are economically feasible.

Actually, researchers are finding that in some cases the cost of retrofitting even a typical two-story residence for energy conservation can be recovered in only a few months. For instance, C. H. Long and John Luoni of the Department of Mechanical Engineering at Virginia Polytechnic Institute & State University discovered that for $557 worth of modifications on a typical Department of Housing and Urban Development (HUD) house, an amazing $464.20 of energy can be saved yearly.

The HUD house was chosen because it represented the typical house found in the Washington, D.C./Baltimore area. The scientists used the Conservation Standard developed by the American Society of Heating, Refrigeration and Air-Conditioning Engineers (ASHRAE 90-75) to check the HUD house in its original form, and more importantly, to check the energy savings brought about by proper retrofitting.

To determine climatic conditions, the scientists used Blacksburg, Virginia weather data. In that town, weather information from 1966 to 1972 was accumulated and reviewed. By using these figures, Long and Luoni broadened their study's application to include possible use in homes in western Virginia, West Virginia, Tennessee, Kentucky, Maryland and even parts of Pennsylvania, Ohio, Indiana and Illinois.

After completing the study, which included analysis of the usefulness and cost of insulation, weatherstripping and storm windows, Long and Luoni discovered that the typical HUD house had an average heating load of 30,920 kilowatt hours, estimated to cost $720 for the average heating season. The average cooling load needed 7,121 kilowatt hours, at an estimated cost of $104.

Using insulation on the ceiling and under the main floor, as well as storm windows and weatherstripping, lowered the heating load to 11,020 kilowatt hours, for a yearly saving of $455. The new cooling load would also be lowered, bringing the total saving to $464.20 annually.

These modifications were relatively minor, costing a mere $557. Luoni and Long calculate that it will take 1.2 years with an eight-percent capital interest rate and a seven-percent fuel cost escalation rate to pay for the modifications, making them well worth the effort.

Insulation Saves Energy

Most Americans are aware of several ways to conserve energy cheaply. Just about every communications medium has hit the public with energy conservation tips, such as lowering our thermostats. Another familiar pointer is to make sure all cracks around doors and windows are sealed tightly. Possibly the most effective energy saver is that simple building material, insulation.

Basically, insulation is characterized by numerous pockets of trapped air distributed throughout its thickness. Because its interlocking fibers are surrounded by lots of air, wood can be the ultimate natural insulator. But solid wood walls, as in log cabins, are fairly expensive, so the primary insulating materials used in home building today are foamed plastics, glass fiber, mineral wool, and fiberboards. Like wood, each of these has the capacity to resist the passage of heat, and all are considerably cheaper than wood to install.

By now you may be wondering how these pockets of air resist heat passage. If you recall high school science, you will remember that heat moves naturally from warmer to cooler surfaces and volumes, based on their temperature differences. If the indoor and outdoor temperatures are within fifteen to twenty degrees of each other, heat transfer is minimal. However, if the temperature difference jumps to sixty degrees, typical of winter days, heat from the house's interior rapidly exits through the exterior walls and roof of uninsulated buildings. The reverse occurs in hot summer months.

As it moves through a wall, heat travels through solid material, such as plaster or gypsum board. This motion is relatively fluid, because the heat hops from one molecule to another with no need to change. When the heat runs into an air pocket, it must change to radiant heat to move across that space. Once it passes through the air pocket, it must again become conducted heat. Each time this occurs, the intensity of the heat diminishes.

As a result, the more separate air spaces heat must traverse, the less actual heat will make it to the outside. Since they consist of thousands of these air pockets or bubbles, foamed plastics, polyurethane and polystyrene are excellent insulators.

Although they may feature a brick or stone facade, most American homes have a basic wood-frame construction. In other words, the walls may be hollow with a three- or four-inch gap and more than a foot of space between each upright member or stud. Similarly, a foot of space often lies between the rafters and joists, or horizontal structural members, of the roof and top-floor ceiling. These spaces are ideal for insertion of insulation.

While heat loss through the roof, walls and floor varies, the roof can lose the most heat, since warm air rises. So the thickest layer of insulation should be installed either in the roof structure or in the floor of the attic, if there is one. Next most important are the exterior walls, followed by flooring that lies above unheated or exposed areas.

Mineral and glass wool insulation are available in paper-wrapped batts or rolls of material, often referred to as blankets, sized to fit tightly between the roof's studs or rafters. Glass wool and mineral wool can also be blown into the attic floor spaces. In some areas of the country, insulation contractors will foam polyurethane into empty wall spaces, without having to remove the interior wall.

Basically, foamed-in insulation requires making a small series of holes in the gypsum board, between the studs in the room-side of an exterior wall. Many building fire codes require fire-resistant barriers for such products as urethane foam. If you opt for this form of insulation, make sure you meet your local building codes.

Another fine insulation material is rigid fiberboard, generally a wood paste or paper that is pressed into four-foot by eight-foot sheets. This form of insulation is available at most lumberyards and home improvement centers.

The most important factor with any kind of insulation is its total thickness. You can even combine three or four different insulation types because roof decking as well as sheathing and siding on the walls and the flooring add insulating values. Today, most manufacturers use an "R rating" to calculate the material's resistance to heat transfer. The higher the R rating, the better the insulating properties of the material.

Since the energy crisis, standards of insulation thickness have been raised considerably. It's important to find out the R value recommended for the various insulation applications, and what thickness will achieve the standard in your particular climate region. For many parts of the country, a total of eight inches or more in the roof is recommended for a resultant R rating of thirty. Walls generally should have four or five inches of insulation, with an R factor of twenty. Exposed floors need a minimum of three inches, or an R value of eight.

Your choice of insulation depends a great deal on its application. For instance, foamed-in insulation is excellent for attics of existing or newly-built houses; however, it can settle in the walls. Batts seem to be best for walls whose interiors have not been finished, so you'll find them used frequently in new construction and major renovation projects. Foamed plastic boards with a new weather surface placed over them are ideal for application to the outside of walls or roofs.

After the insulation is installed, some other items should be considered. With the exception of foamed plastics, which do not absorb water, insulation must be kept dry. Wet insulation will not resist heat transfer effectively, so all surfaces exposed to the elements must be watertight. When possible, air should be able to circulate around the batts or blankets of insulation. A vapor barrier on the room-side of the exterior wall also may be necessary.

You should also make sure that windows and doors have insulating glass or storm sashes, especially on those sides of the house that are blasted by winter winds. All cracks around doors and windows should be sealed. One good indicator of effective insulation in these areas is whether or not a window needs to be opened occasionally in the winter to remove excess moisture from cooking areas or showers. Although such humidity can be annoying after a shower, it indicates that your room is well insulated.

While the reduction of both fuel consumption and costs are prime motivators for insulating your home today, there are also other reasons. Drafts and cold floors, such as in tiled playrooms or family rooms, can be controlled through good insulation. The more appropriate the insulation and weatherproofing incorporated into your house, the more comfortable it will be when you move in.

In addition, your home's energy efficiency can make or break a future sale or rental of your house. Today's buyers are more likely to ask to see your heating and/or cooling bills before they consider your house. With present day costs and future energy escalations, no one wants a poorly insulated home.

The best time to have insulation installed in most parts of the country is in the early spring. During this period of time contractors are often looking for work and haven't yet signed up to handle more extensive jobs. Because the cost of the insulation remains fairly constant, you save money when labor is cheapest.

If you plan to hire a contractor yourself to install the insulation, ask him about the different alternatives and his cost estimates for installing each type. You should talk to more than one contractor to get the best bid for the installation.

Ask employees of lumberyards or home improvement centers for names of qualified insulation installers. Then query the installers for the names of customers whose experiences in fuel savings can be checked.

For the more adventuresome, insulation and weatherproofing can be do-it-yourself projects. Most forms of insulation can be installed in simple stages that require little or no technical knowledge.

Window Placement
When properly used and located, window designs can offer comfort and economy, without penalizing you with extremely high energy bills. A single pane of glass has a thermal or heat conductivity, or an R rating, of 0.88. An insulated wall often has an R rating of nineteen. In other words, the heat flow through one square foot of window is equal to the heat flowing through twenty-one square feet of insulated wall.

In many cold regions, double glazing (two sheets of glass separated by an air pocket) has helped reduce heat loss. For properly spaced layers of glass, the heat flow comparison between window and insulated wall drops to about 11 square feet per square foot of window. In some states, such as Illinois and Wisconsin, concerned builders recommend triple glazing to reduce heat loss; in Alaska, the coldest state in the Union, quadruple glazing is sometimes chosen.

One of the most critical factors of windows is their vulnerability to solar radiation. As much as ninety percent of the sun's heat can be transmitted through glass during the summer months. For this reason, a number of architects and contractors recommend the use of very small windows on the east and west sides of the house. Some even recommend no windows at all. During one hour on a hot summer day, an east or west window can admit as much heat through one square foot as through 225 square feet of insulated wall!

During the summer, south windows can be easily protected from direct solar heat with roof projections or overhangs, because the mid-day sun, which is the hottest, has a high vertical angle during this season. In the winter, the sun is at a lower angle. Even when the temperature outside is thirty-two degrees Fahrenheit on a clear day, the sun can heat the interior to seventy-seven degrees through the south windows.

Studying the effects of what scientists call passive solar features, researchers measured the power costs of two separate houses in Davis, California. One house was designed to take advantage of sun angles, while the other house, which was not particularly vulnerable from the east and west, lacked the valuable south-side windows. University of California scientists found major cost and energy usage differences between the two houses.

For the house designed to use glass properly for energy savings, the power costs amounted to $65 for seven months. The other house ran up a $286 bill for the same period. "In Davis, with a population of approximately 33,000, and homes numbering about 11,000—if all were to convert to passive solar features with proper size and orientation of windows—an annual savings of about $2.4 million might be expected," noted Loren W. Neubauer of the University of California.

For those who thrive in bright, sunlit rooms, the idea of eliminating all east and west windows paints a dark picture. But energy-conscious homeowners need not despair. East windows generally only provide bright light during the early hours of the day, while west windows offer only afternoon light. And this small amount of extra sunshine really doesn't justify the accompanying heat transfer. North windows, on the other hand, are the least useful, providing minimal light and heat. This brings us once again to the south windows, which can be increased in size or number to compensate for elimination of windows on the other sides of the house. Also, as plant lovers know, south windows are greenery's best friends.

Research shows that south rooms with large windows actually can be solar-heated as high as one hundred and four degrees Fahrenheit on cold winter days, while with proper soffit projection, the same windows can keep the room at about seventy-seven degrees in the summer without air conditioning!

When these solar principles are applied, energy savings in both the summer and the winter can exceed fifty to eighty percent, with no extra cost in building design or orientation.

If you are interested in conserving energy through windows, you may wish to familiarize yourself with the following types of glass.

Usually called window glass, *float glass* is poured flat, then cooled slowly to reduce its brittleness. Common, single-strength glass is 3/32-inch thick, while double-strength is 1/8-inch thick.

Plate glass actually is thicker float glass. While regular plate glass is often 1/4-inch thick, thicker plates are also available.

Tempered glass is about five times stronger than conventional glass. It gets its name from the process by which it is made—heating and cooling. Many building codes require this type of glass for all doors and hazardous locations, since when it does break, the glass crumbles into small pebbles, rather than splintering as conventional glass does. Because it cannot be cut, ground or drilled, tempered glass is available only in standard sizes, unless custom designed and prepared.

Safety glass actually is two panes of glass sandwiched around a layer of plastic. When the glass is broken, the plastic interlayer holds the fragments together. Safety glass can be cut to fit nonstandard sizes and shapes for homes.

Wired glass is often used for skylights. It features a diamond-patterned mesh that is embedded into the glass to hold glass particles together if the glass is broken.

Heat-absorbing glass is also called solar glass. Frequently offered in green, gray or bronze tints that vary in opacity, this glass type can absorb solar heat.

Reflective glass features a mirrorlike coating of transparent metallic oxide in one of several densities. This metallic oxide is fired onto the surface of ¼-inch thick plate glass to reflect up to seventy percent of solar heat and also to cut light transmission by up to fifty percent. Some reflective glass also is called solar glass. You'll have no trouble finding out which has both characteristics, since most companies are quick to point out any energy savings offered by their product.

Patterned glass is passed through patterned rollers that create texture, ribbing and other surface effects.

Insulating glass is also called thermal or double glazed glass. It actually is two or more pieces of glass with a space in between. This air space between the glass layers acts as insulation to reduce heat gain and loss.

The Heat Pump
Although a number of exotic energy saving systems are available to homeowners—methane generators and wind-powered electricity among them—these are not yet in widespread use. Many of them also have mechanical or engineering bugs that you might not want to be concerned with in your own home.

One newer alternative a number of Westerners are using in home building, however, is the heat pump. Essentially, the heat pump moves heat from the cold outdoors to the warmer indoors. This may sound like something conjured up by the wand of Merlin, but the principle it works on is no more fantastic than your central air conditioner. (Some manufacturers also refer to the heat pump as a heat extractor or an energy recovery device.) The heat pump even looks like a central air conditioner. Functionally, that's what it is: an air conditioner that heats rather than cools. To understand how the system works, you need to know these simple physics principles: Heat energy flows naturally from a warmer place to a cooler one. Gases become colder when they are forced to expand. When those same gases are compressed into a smaller space, they become hotter.

Like your air conditioner or refrigerator, the heat pump features a closed loop of refrigerant gas that circulates through two coils, one located inside the house, the other outside. To move air across its surface, each coil has a blower fan. Because the refrigerant is volatile (but not necessarily explosive) it is able to boil from a liquid to a vapor at low temperatures. On one side of the refrigerant loop is an electric compressor. On the other side is a refrigerant expansion valve.

During winter heating, refrigerant gas passes through the expansion valve, where it expands and becomes cooler as it approaches the outside coil. Because the gas is generally colder than the outside air, atmospheric heat moves into the gas through the coil, boiling the liquid into a vapor. Then the vapor is squeezed down by the compressor, making it both hotter and denser. By the time it reaches the indoor coil, the vapor is warmer than the inside of your house.

From the indoor coil, a blower carries the heat away from the hot gas and circulates the warmer air through a normal air duct system. As the gas loses heat, it condenses to a liquid again and returns through the expansion valve to recirculate through the system.

During the warm summer months, a thermostat reverses this refrigerant flow. In other words, it captures indoor heat through the indoor coil, then moves through the compressor, dispersing the heat outdoors. This principle really is behind your air conditioner's operation. Contrary to what you might think, an air conditioner doesn't create cold air. It extracts heat from the air and leaves cooler air inside your home.

Climate conditions, local sources of energy, and your current heating system determine whether or not you can use a heat pump. Modern heat pumps are sophisticated machines that can cost approximately twenty-five percent more than a standard furnace and air conditioner. Including new ducts, a heat pump may cost between $2,000 and $3,000 for the entire package. The important thing to keep in mind is whether or not this investment can be justified by lower heating and cooling costs.

For areas of the country where the regulated price of natural gas is low, a heat pump is not likely to pay for itself as compared to a conventional gas furnace and electric air conditioner. However, the heat pump does pay off when compared to oil or propane heating and air conditioning. As electricity rates continue to rise, the heat pump may also be able to compete favorably with electric heating.

The heat pump has a few snags. As temperatures drop below thirty-five to forty degrees Fahrenheit, the heat pump may need backup electrical assistance in heating. Consequently, heat pumps are best for houses in the West or South, not in the snow belt. If you have long winters and you can count on seeing snow, a heat pump probably isn't your best bet.

Since a heat pump is more complex than other air handling equipment, the dealer or contractor who installs it should be certified by the manufacturer. Some local utility companies may supply you with the names of manufacturer-certified dealers. Others will help you calculate the life-cycle costs of a heat pump as compared with other heating and cooling systems.

For colder areas of the country, most manufacturers recommend sizing the system for cooling needs, with a backup heating system to meet extra heating needs in the winter. A large system designed for heating might be too large for cooling and end up costing you more, cooling inefficiently and providing poor humidity control.

Heat pumps are measured by tonnage. A ton is 12,000 BTUs per hour of heat removed from the home. A three-ton unit, for example, could be adequate for a 1,500-square-foot house when the outside temperature stays higher than thirty-five degrees.

Because the heat delivered by a heat pump reaches the room at about one hundred degrees rather than at the one hundred twenty-five degrees provided by more conventional furnaces, a heat pump requires larger ductwork and more registers. And since the heat is lower in temperature, your home must also be well insulated.

Housed in the shell of the outside coil unit are the compressor, expansion valve and other components. To avoid neighborhood complaints and sleepless nights yourself, stay away from installing the unit near bedrooms, walls or your neighbor's property line. The unit also needs to be protected from standing water, snow drifts and gale-force winds. To prevent infiltration of ground water, you could mount the unit on a concrete slab. At the same time, the heat pump needs free air circulating around it. Generally, locating the unit on the west or south side of your home provides the best heat source, since those areas are subjected to more winter winds.

Heat pumps also are frequently teamed up with solar collectors. (For further information, see the chapter on solar energy systems.) Solar collectors work best on clear, sunny, winter days, while heat pumps can provide heat on the cloudier, and often warmer winter days when solar collectors are less effective.

Whether or not you opt for the heat pump, you will need to consider energy in building your home. Cheap and plentiful sources of energy that once allowed Americans to take household comfort for granted are rapidly diminishing. As more people realize that energy costs are not going to come down, they will begin tightening up their houses.

Chapter 5
Harnessing the Sun

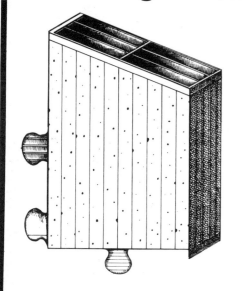

Although no one has compiled a complete list of existing solar energy applications in the U.S., informed industry sources suggest that there are approximately 2,000 solar-heated buildings. Within twenty-five years, experts estimate, several million solar heating systems will be in use in this country, replacing about one hundred million barrels of imported oil!

Most industry experts agree that space heating and hot water heating are the two major functions at which solar energy has been proven effective. Other applications, such as solar cooling systems, are now on the drawing boards; authorities consider future possibilities almost unlimited. Since hot water loads are relatively insensitive to outdoor temperatures or conditions, they can be provided throughout the year. Space heating homes is much trickier.

Actually, an *active* solar system should be the last move you make in the whole series of energy saving steps. First of all, you should make sure that any home you buy is properly "winterized." Next, you need to incorporate passive design features such as southern exposure, double-glazed windows for winter heat conservation, insulating shades and overhangs for summer shading. In fact, if you follow all of the tips listed in Chapter 4, you'll have a complete *passive* energy-saving system. If the house you plan to purchase already has such features, you may want to consider installing an active solar system designed for your particular region of the country.

Almost any style house will lend itself to a solar energy system. Solar energy homes can be custom built or prefabricated; they even are beginning to crop up in more creative subdivisions. Styles range from contemporary to traditional, but one important thing to remember is that these homes were designed specifically to handle solar energy. Houses are tightly built from an energy conservation standpoint, and they are properly oriented on the site for the solar collectors.

Although the earlier solar energy homes flaunted the solar collectors, more modern designs play them down. They may be integrated in the roofing system or along one exterior wall.

Some builders find that with only minor modifications they can easily integrate solar energy systems into their standard model plans. Others design the homes completely with solar energy in mind. Cost estimates for incorporating solar energy into housing are not as prohibitive as they once were. Builders estimate that solar energy can be woven into the house design for between $5,000 and $10,000, depending on the system and the overall house design.

One Wisconsin builder incorporated a solar system into the rear elevation of a 1,000-square-foot prefabricated house. (You'll hear building professionals use the term *elevation* when referring to a side, or exterior wall, of your house.) The solar equipment and installation added approximately $6 per square foot to the $43,000 house. An identical house without solar energy systems was built across the street. With electric baseboard heating, the nonsolar house received a typical heating bill of $150. During the same winter, the solar house's heating bill was a mere $30.

As solar homes become more attractive both economically and physically, buyers are asking some important questions—the most important of which is whether or not it pays to equip a house with a solar system. The answer depends on a number of variables, including location, utility costs and the type of solar system. Eventually, the monitored HUD solar grant homes will provide a concrete answer. In the meantime, solar homeowners are finding proof of the savings in their heating bills.

In New Mexico, one $9,000 solar system, including extra insulation, provides about seventy-five percent of the heat and ninety percent of the home's hot water. In California, a combination of insulation and an active solar system fulfills more than ninety percent of the heating requirements of a 1,500-square-foot home. In

Ohio, a traditional housing model with solar collectors and heavy insulation—R-20 in the walls and R-36 in the ceiling—is estimated to provide fifty percent of the heat and seventy percent of the hot water. The solar system in this house, which is being monitored under the HUD solar grant program, cost $9,000.

Since the solar industry is still in its infancy, new systems and builders are constantly entering the market. For lists of builders who are currently constructing solar homes as well as the names of companies marketing solar heating and cooling equipment, write the National Solar Heating and Cooling Information Center, P.O. Box 1607, Rockville, Maryland.

Understanding How Solar Energy Works
To understand how a solar energy system works, let's look at the Solar Cape design offered by Acorn Structures of Concord, Massachusetts. Through the winter of 1975–76, a solar system provided forty-six percent of the space heating required for Acorn's 1,400-square-foot Village House (one of several prefab styles the company offers).

In this system, the solar collectors are built to serve as roofing panels as well. They are available in a four-foot by twenty-foot size, minimizing piping connections, flashing and jointing. Each panel features an exterior polyester and glass fiber glazing cover and frame, a copper tubing grid with a black-painted aluminum fin-plate absorbing surface, followed by two inches of glass fiber insulation, waterproofing membrane and a half-inch thick fir plywood backing that serves as roof sheathing. The black-painted collector plate absorbs sunlight energy. The plastic-glazed cover protects the absorbing surface from heat loss due to wind and cold air.

The heat absorbed by the collector plates is transferred to water circulated from a storage tank, similar to the process used by the hot water coil in a stove or furnace. Storage of collected solar energy is provided by a wood-framed, vinyl-lined and insulated 2,200-gallon water tank. When fully charged by the sun, the tank contains enough energy to heat a house for several days.

By pumping the warm storage water through a coil placed in the duct of the warm air heating system, collected and stored heat is transferred from the tank into the house. While the water could be pumped through hot water baseboard radiators, the coil in the duct with a warm air system can have certain advantages. For instance, the system can be more tightly designed, since the air flow rate can be controlled. Also, by placing the water coil upstream of the back-up heat source, the two systems can interface and work together without special controls. For greatest economy in operating costs and fuel consumption, Acorn recommends an oil-fired warm air furnace to supply back-up space heating.

In the Solar Cape house, heat is controlled by a two-stage thermostat. When the house cools to the first stage setting, the thermostat activates the air circulation fan and the pump. As it moves through the coil, air is warmed by the water in the solar storage tank and heats the house. If the storage water is not warm enough to satisfy the thermostat, the house cools to the second stage. At this point, the back-up furnace is activated by the thermostat. However, the back-up furnace runs only until it reaches the second setting on the thermometer. Thus, the solar system interacts with the furnace in heating the house.

In the dead of winter, when the solar energy is rapidly consumed, the air circulation fan and the pump will run for long periods of time. Don't be too concerned about the expense, because the fan does not consume much electricity and it helps to distribute the passive solar heat that may be entering through the south windows on sunny days. This prevents rooms that receive considerable passive solar heat through windows from becoming overheated, because that heat is being distributed throughout your house.

At this point, a further distinction should be made between active and passive solar systems.

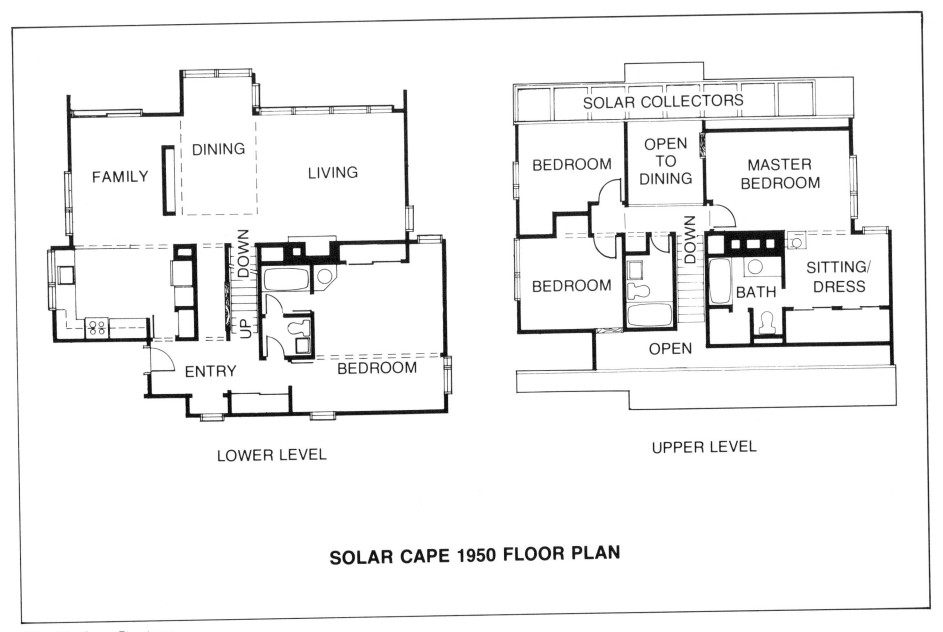

LOWER LEVEL

UPPER LEVEL

Lower Level labels: FAMILY, DINING, LIVING, DOWN, UP, ENTRY, BEDROOM

Upper Level labels: SOLAR COLLECTORS, BEDROOM, OPEN TO DINING, MASTER BEDROOM, DOWN, BEDROOM, BATH, SITTING/DRESS, OPEN

SOLAR CAPE 1950 FLOOR PLAN

Offered by Acorn Structures, Inc., this solar collector home's floor plan features bedrooms on the upper level and living and entertaining areas on the ground floor. Drawing by Ken Nash

37

An active system uses collectors and relies on mechanical power to move the heat. These systems use either air or water to carry the heat from the collectors to the storage area and then out through the living areas of the house. Passive systems, on the other hand, use the complete house structure as both the collection and storage media. Through well-designed windows, the sun's heat rays enter the home during the winter. Then massive internal structures, frequently concrete floors and adobe or concete walls, absorb the heat and gradually release it when the sun goes down. Sometimes movable flaps or wall panels are used to direct the heat through the house. Insulating shutters also limit the escape of heat through the home's windows.

Like many other active solar energy designs, the Solar Cape home incorporates both the active solar collectors and certain passive solar features to make the overall solar power more effective. The solar collector in the home is controlled by a thermal switch that turns on the pump feeding the storage tank, when the collector is warm enough to add heat to the already stored water. When this pump is off, the water drains out of the collector and back into the storage tank so that it won't lose energy or freeze during the winter.

Domestic hot water also gets its heat from the system by passing through a forty-gallon preheating tank, which is submerged in the storage water, and on to the hot water heater. In the summer months, when the solar collectors are not heating the house, they supply sufficient energy to carry almost all of the hot water heating load. During the winter, when the storage tank is being used to heat the home, this tank still heats the cold incoming water to approximately seventy-five degrees Fahrenheit. Although the water will have to be heated further by an electric heater from the preheating tank, it is still taking off much of the water's initial chill, lowering the energy costs for hot water heat.

Collectors and Tudor Mix

In Plano, Texas there sits a house featuring English Tudor styling that easily blends with other homes in the neighborhood. The difference is that the Solarmate Home features solar collectors, a heat pump and energy efficiency along with its traditional styling. From the front view, you might notice that the windows are carefully placed. From the rear you will note fourteen solar collector panels mounted on the roof's southern exposure. To provide shade around the second-story window and to accommodate the solar panels, the roof features an extra-long overhang.

To heat the home, twelve solar collectors assist a two-speed heat pump. The other two collectors provide heat for the domestic hot water supply. Along with the heat pump, the solar collectors, hot water heater and monitoring equipment make up a complete package of energy-saving gear from Lennox Industries, Inc., of Marshalltown, Iowa.

Depending on the amount of solar energy collected and the heating requirements of the home, the system operates in different phases. The solar energy phase of the system uses an antifreeze solution, pumped up into the collecting panels on the roof. While the antifreeze solution circulates through the solar panels, it collects heat. On sunny days, the solution reaches about 250 degrees Fahrenheit. Then it is pumped through a heat exchanger in the 500-gallon storage tank. The heat exchanger transfers the heat in the antifreeze into the water in the storage tank, where the water is stored until it is needed to heat the home.

When the water temperature in the storage tank is high enough, and when the home needs the heat, a second heat exchanger located at the top of the storage tank transfers the stored heat into a liquid in the system. This liquid then travels through a hydronic coil in the furnace. Air blown over the coil is heated and circulated throughout the home via heat ducts.

Designed by William Styczynski, this house was planned for a middle-income Chicago family, and for a typically confined urban site. Photo: William Styczynski.

Built and designed by Fitch
Creations Inc. . . . the
"Homemade" Solar System
provides 60 to 80% of the heat
and hot water for 1400 square
foot house.
Photo: American Plywood Association

Architect Barry Berkus did
the Solar Collectors in this design in the parapet.
Photo: Professional Builder

On moderately cold days or after several days of cloudiness, another phase of the system activates. Since the temperature of the water in the solar energy storage tank may not be warm enough to heat the house, the liquid is routed through a heat pump instead of going directly through the hydronic coil. Acting as a refrigerator in reverse, the heat pump extracts heat from the outside air and warms the liquid to the temperature necessary to heat the home. On cool fall days, the heat pump can extract enough heat from the air to heat the house. However, when the temperature dips below freezing and stays there, an electric resistance-heating unit in the furnace is used to heat the house.

Keeping all of this equipment running efficiently is the function of the monitoring equipment. This equipment automatically keeps track of all temperatures and heat requirements, switching from one phase to another as needed.

Financing Solar Systems

Although shopping for financing will not be easy, you should be able to get a conventional twenty-five-year mortgage on your solar energy home from a lending institution. In 1978, nearly forty percent of the nation's home mortgage lenders used energy-saving information in their advertising and marketing efforts, according to a survey of the Savings Institutions Marketing Society of America. The results of that survey indicate that many lenders now realize that energy efficiency is important, not only because future energy supplies are uncertain, but also because home energy efficiency is increasingly important to family budgeting decisions.

As with every other aspect of solar energy systems, financing is in a state of flux. The possibilities for financing solar additions to existing homes are even less clear-cut than for new solar homes. At the time this book went to press, legislation was pending that would give tax breaks to homeowners who retrofit their houses for energy conservation. The 1977 Federal Income Tax

Form 1040A carried this notice:

At the time . . . these instructions were printed, Congress was considering legislation that would allow credits for energy saving expenses for your personal residence. If this legislation is passed and you had such expenses, you must file Form 1040—not Form 1040A—to claim the credits.

If this legislation is passed, more financing opportunities should open up for homeowners making such modifications.

You probably will have to shop around to get good mortgage financing for a solar energy home. You may be required to have your architect supply you with detailed plans and specifications to show the lender.

As in any other major purchase, research the companies you deal with before you agree to anything. Solar energy is a burgeoning market, and there could be some less-than-reputable companies that were formed just to collect the unwitting buyer's dollars, with little or no attention paid to delivering or installing solar panels.

Even if you are considering buying a pre-engineered or prefabricated solar home (and there are some very nice ones on the market), you should hire a local architect at least as an independent consultant to review the plans and specifications before you buy the home.

An active solar system with solar collectors will collect the same amount of energy even if the house is not efficiently designed and well constructed. However, since conserving heat, and not collecting it, is the most important factor, the house should be designed to benefit as much as possible from solar heating, with minimal heat loss through the walls, roof, floors and the windows. (See Making Your House Snug, Chapter 4, for details.)

Maximum insulation should be used in the walls, roof and floors. You should also have at least double-glazed or insulated glass throughout

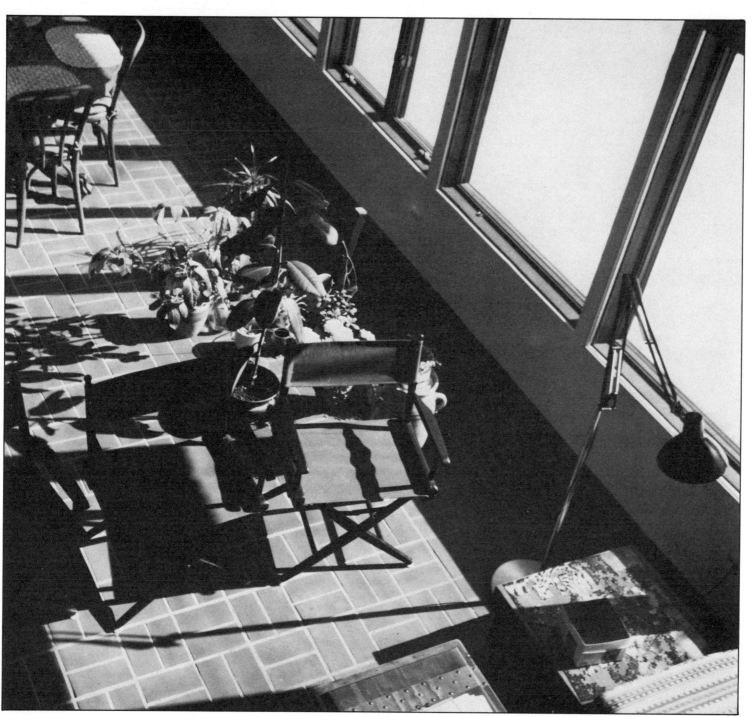

Left and facing page:
An example of passive solar features, this house by Roger G. Whitmer, A.I.A., features optimum south windows and provision for an active solar collector system retrofit. Photo: Roger G. Whitmer.

Harnessing the Sun

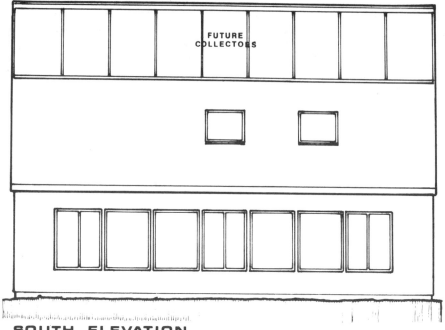

SOUTH ELEVATION

FUTURE COLLECTORS

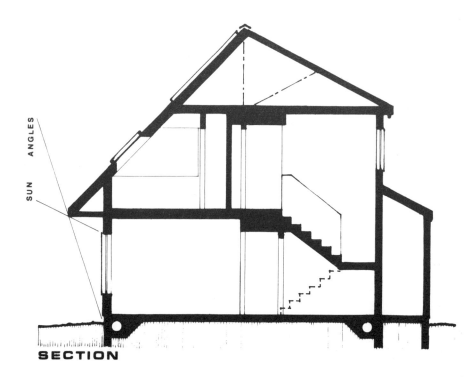

SECTION

SUN ANGLES

Right and facing page:

Elevation, section, and floor plans for Roger Whitmer's house with passive solar features.

Courtesy of Roger G. Whitmer, A.I.A.

0   4   8   12

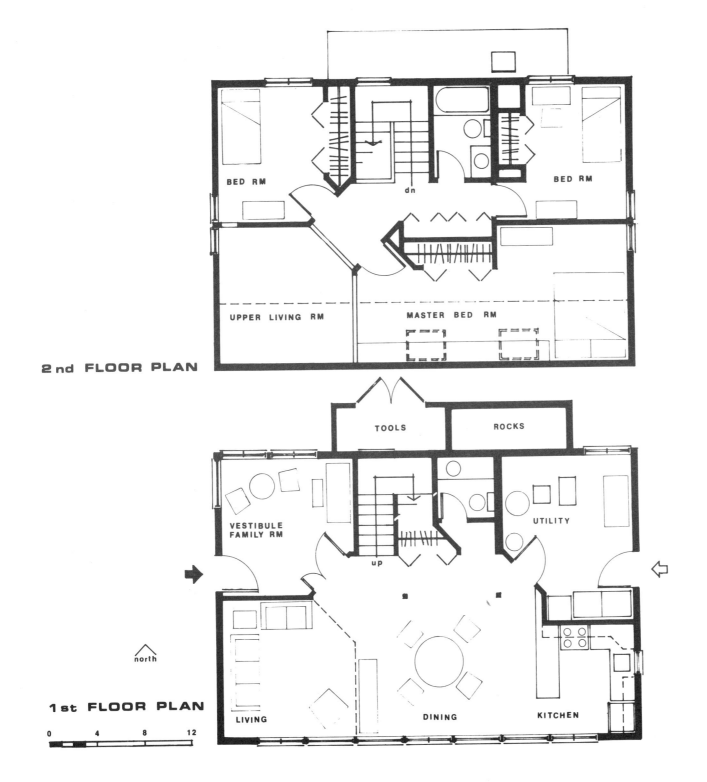

2nd FLOOR PLAN

BED RM

dn

BED RM

UPPER LIVING RM

MASTER BED RM

TOOLS

ROCKS

VESTIBULE
FAMILY RM

up

UTILITY

north

1st FLOOR PLAN

0   4   8   12

LIVING

DINING

KITCHEN

45

the house. Windows and doors should be tightly weatherstripped.

Most solar designs minimize windows on the north exposures and maximize glass on the south-facing side, with protective overhangs to guard against too much heat penetration from the summer sun. Generally, the living areas of the home are located along this south side to take advantage of the windows.

Bedrooms and corridors often are located on the north sides or the top floor of the solar energy home, so they can be zoned separately and regulated at lower temperatures. If the house has an indoor fireplace, the chimney often will be placed in the middle rather than on one side of the home, so that you can benefit from the heat generated in the smoke stack. Entries generally are designed so that they can protect the living areas from a direct influx of cold air.

Although a solar system significantly increases the cost of a new home, it may provide the answer for anyone who wants to conserve energy and has the ability to finance it.

Talking the Solar Language
People who are used to talking about solar energy have a language of their own. Here are some of the more frequently used terms and what they mean:

Absorptance is measured as a percentage of the total radiation available. Absorptance is the absorption of heat by a solar collector.

Absorption refrigeration is a cooling system that is operated by solar-heated hot water instead of a mechanical compressor.

Bead wall actually is a simple and effective method of insulating glass. Styrene foam beads are placed into the air space between a double glass wall. During the day, these beads are pumped out to allow the sun's rays to enter and heat the house. At night, the beads are pumped back into the glass walls, to act as insulation. More sophisticated than double-glazing, bead walls enable homeowners to install a glorious pic-

ture window without paying through the nose for energy loss.

Bio fuels are renewable energy sources from living things, their by-products and wastes.

Bioconversion is the conversion of solar energy into fuel by plants and algae. This term is also found in connection with such less conventional fuel sources as methane gas products.

British thermal unit, or *BTU*, is the amount of energy required to heat one pound of water one degree Fahrenheit.

Collector tilt is the angle at which a solar collector is positioned to face the sun for best solar collection.

Concentrator is a reflector or lens that is designed to focus a large amount of sunshine into a small area, which increases the temperature and makes the solar collector work more effectively.

Emittance is the amount of heat radiated back from the solar collector. It is measured as a percentage of the energy absorbed by the collector.

Flat-plate collector is a panel of metal or other soluble material that converts sunlight into heat. Frequently a flat black color, the collector then transfers its heat either to recirculating air or to water, depending on the total solar energy system used.

Fresnel lens is a thin lens of glass or plastic that serves as a concentrator of sunlight.

Glauber's salt is an inexpensive substance that can be used for storing solar heat. When the salt melts, it absorbs a large amount of heat that can be released later for nighttime heating.

Heliostat is a fixed mirror that is used to reflect the sun's rays into a solar collector.

Insolation is the amount of solar radiation received.

Kilowatt is equal to approximately 1-1/3 horsepower. Literally, it is one thousand watts of power.

Langley is a unit of measurement of insulation. A langley equals one gram-calorie per square centimeter.

Megawatt is one million watts, or one

This passive solar design collects solar heat without solar collectors. Located in Seattle, the design consists of a sun spa incorporated into a standard 1,900 square foot house. Photo: American Plywood Association

This private residence in De-Kalb, Illinois, incorporates a solar roof built on-site, south-facing windows for direct solar gain in winter, and an overhanging roof for shade in summer. It was designed by the Hawkweed Group, Ltd.

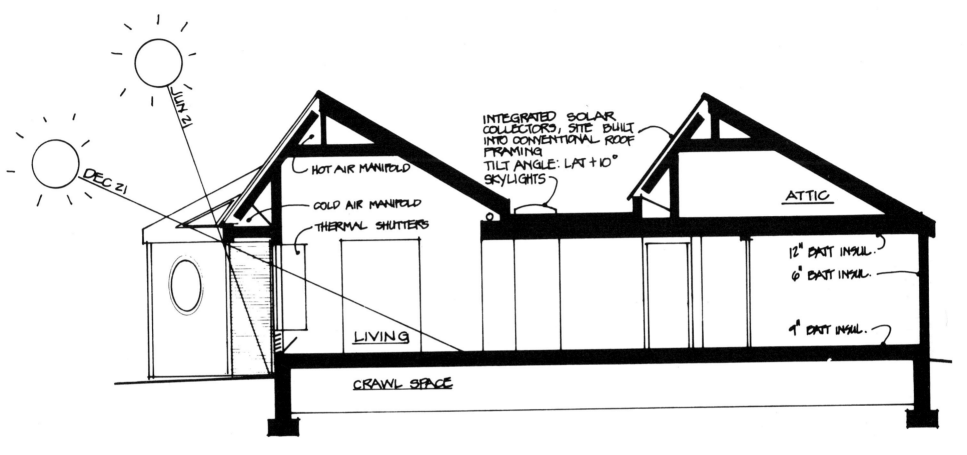

JUN 21

DEC 21

HOT AIR MANIFOLD

COLD AIR MANIFOLD

THERMAL SHUTTERS

INTEGRATED SOLAR COLLECTORS, SITE BUILT INTO CONVENTIONAL ROOF FRAMING
TILT ANGLE: LAT + 10°
SKYLIGHTS

ATTIC

12" BATT INSUL.

6" BATT INSUL.

4" BATT INSUL.

LIVING

CRAWL SPACE

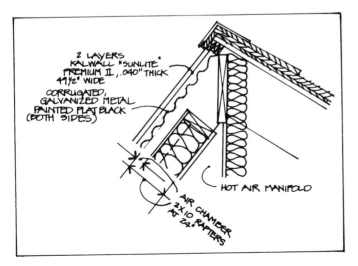

2 LAYERS KALWALL "SUNLITE" PREMIUM II , .040" THICK 49½" WIDE

CORRUGATED, GALVANIZED METAL PAINTED FLAT BLACK (BOTH SIDES)

AIR CHAMBER 2 X 10 RAFTERS AT 24"

HOT AIR MANIFOLD

SECTION

0 1 2   4   8   16 FEET

This page and overleaf:

Section drawings for the Hawkweed Group's solar-heated residence in DeKalb, Illinois. Courtesy of the Hawkweed Group

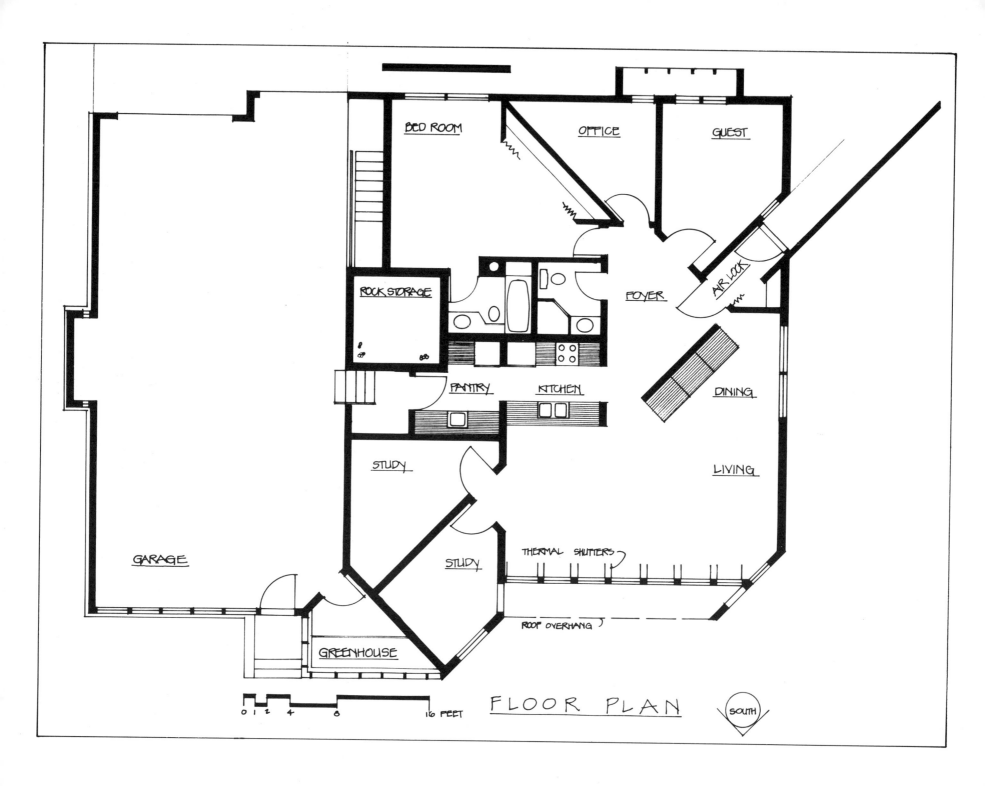

BED ROOM

OFFICE

GUEST

ROCK STORAGE

FOYER

AIR LOCK

PANTRY

KITCHEN

DINING

STUDY

LIVING

GARAGE

STUDY

THERMAL SHUTTERS

ROOF OVERHANG

GREENHOUSE

0 1 2 4   8   16 FEET

FLOOR PLAN

SOUTH

Chapter 6
Underground Housing— Returning to Our Roots

For thousands of years, man took advantage of the earth's natural elements for housing. Caves offered protection from the rain and snow. They also offered privacy. As man grew more sophisticated, he emerged from the caves and began building his home above ground. The new homes, however, were not as easily heated, so *Homo sapiens* developed indoor fire, later followed by complete indoor heating and cooling systems.

Today the heating and cooling fuels once thought infinitely available are becoming scarce, so some Americans are retracing their housing roots by living in underground or berm homes. For the truly energy-conscious, underground living is both the oldest and the newest form of alternate housing.

The sites of existing underground or berm houses are scattered from Texas to Massachusetts and from Florida to California. Going underground is proving successful in a wide variety of climates and environments. Underground housing means low fuel bills, low maintenance and probably the ultimate in privacy and security. The concept is becoming increasingly popular on college campuses such as the University of Minnesota, Arizona State University, the University of Texas and the University of New Mexico. Concerned scientists and students at these institutions are rediscovering the advantages of underground living for today's sophisticated family.

Only a decade ago, anyone who seriously considered burying their family's home six feet under probably would have been quietly committed to a mental institution. But while the concept is still in its experimental stages, underground housing is beginning to gain the respect of serious researchers who are looking for viable alternatives in housing. Even the National Science Foundation (NSF) has gotten into the act of providing funds for research projects.

The primary attraction of underground housing seems to stem from the home's inherent energy savings. Not very far beneath the ground surface of your own back yard, the temperature of the earth stays relatively constant. Depending on your overall climatic temperature variance, underground temperature hovers around fifty degrees Fahrenheit, despite whether above-ground temperatures reach ninety-five degrees in the shade or minus ten degrees when the wind doesn't howl.

That stable, moderate temperature helps to explain the major advantage of building underground: you can save enormously on heating and cooling costs. Although some underground homes also incorporate solar collectors, you normally don't need exotic technology to heat and cool an underground or berm house.

There are other advantages, too. Since the building itself takes up little ground surface area, grass and wildflowers can become your roof. You experience an amazing sense of seclusion and quiet. You virtually eliminate the external maintenance of your house, with the possible exception of summertime, when you may wish to mow your roof. Underground housing isn't threatened by storms and tornados, although floods might not be too pleasant.

For those whose creative urges are not fulfilled by painting the house or patching the roof, underground houses offer a special bonus. While you might still need step ladders and other basic tools for interior repairs, you can often avoid the clutter of extension ladders, half-empty paint cans and other tools used in external maintenance. If you're the gardener rather than the handyman type, you'll really be in your element. Rather than cleaning leaves out of your gutter, you can spend your time weeding and planting the roof; your principal exterior maintenance gear could be a rake, a hoe and a shovel.

With all of these advantages, it's little wonder that mankind is returning to its roots and the good green earth overhead. Though there still are only a few underground homes in the U.S., vast communities already have gone underground to avoid the scorching heat of Australia,

Underground Housing—
Returning to Our Roots

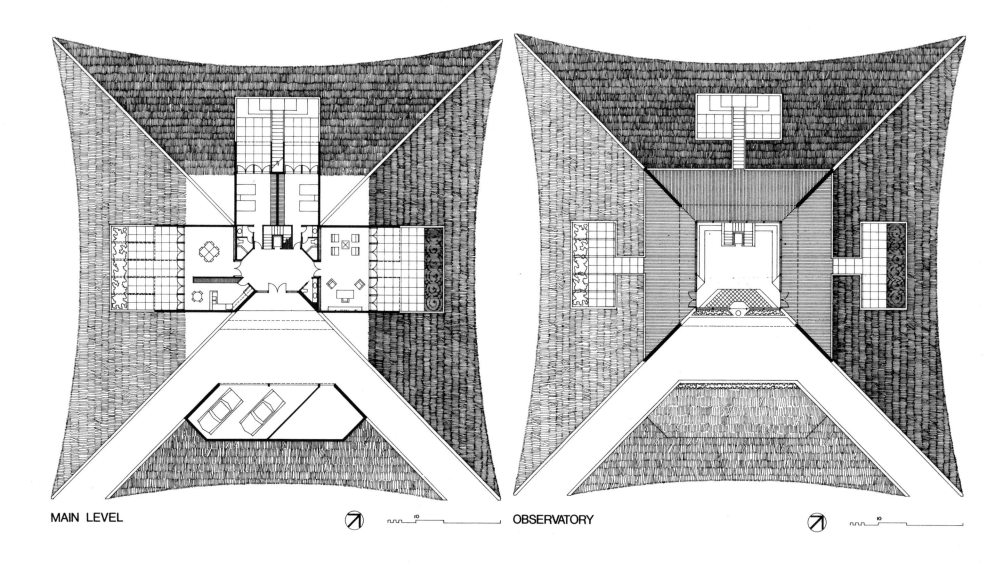

MAIN LEVEL

OBSERVATORY

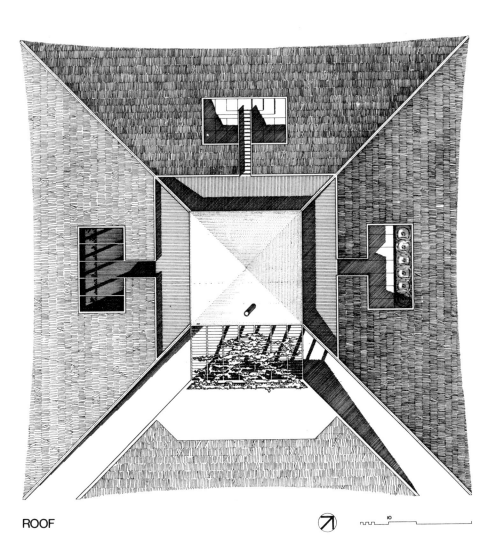

ROOF

Presentation drawings for
William Morgan's central
Florida Hilltop Residence.

Courtesy of William Morgan,
A.I.A.

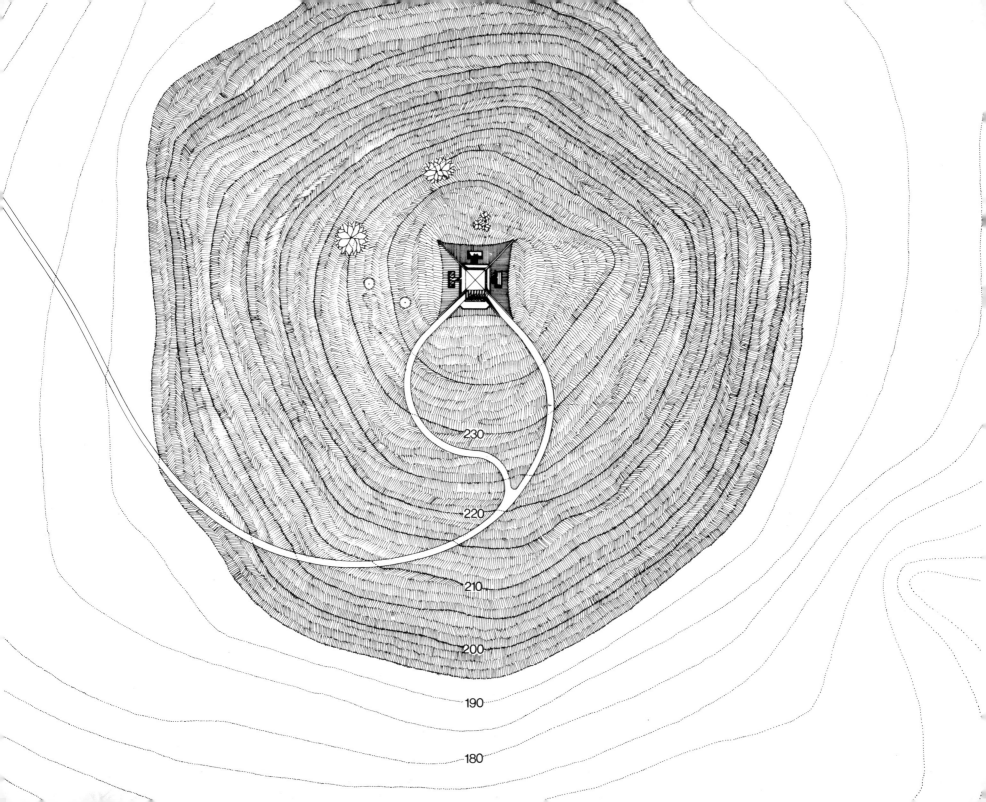

SECTION

10

This and facing page:

Presentation drawings for
William Morgan's central
Florida Hilltop Residence.

Underground Housing— Returning to Our Roots

Tunisia and Spain, or the frigid winds of northern China.

The question is: can you, a window-crazed, high-rise dweller in love with the "fresh air" of car exhausts make the transition to underground living? As a number of people are discovering, yes, you can.

Earth-sheltered houses come in a variety of forms. Some are built into hillsides. Others are constructed partially underground; these are called berm houses. The ultimate underground home is built entirely underground. The main feature of all types of underground construction is the use of soil surrounding the structure as insulation.

Anyone familiar with a basement knows that underground space is warmer than the outside air in winter and cooler in the summer. That's because most buildings lose heat through the walls and roof. Since an underground house has relatively few exposed surfaces, it is not subject to the high energy losses that conventional homes experience through windows, and since the earth around the house is also fairly stable in temperature, heat loss through the walls also is reduced drastically as compared to other forms of housing.

Although you might have to dig pretty deep to find earth at a constant fifty degrees Fahrenheit, ground temperatures at depths as shallow as one to ten feet are much less changeable than surface temperatures. Daily fluctuations in air temperature do not affect the soil temperature at all. Even monthly changes in ground temperature are considerably behind the temperature changes you feel when you go outdoors.

To illustrate this point, Dr. Thomas Bligh of the Mechanical Engineering Department at the University of Minnesota measured the underground temperature in the St. Paul-Minneapolis area. He found the Twin Cities' surface temperatures vary from a frigid minus thirty-five degrees Fahrenheit to an amazing ninety-five degrees, a 125 degree variance. However, when Bligh measured the underground temperature in the same area he found that it ranged from about forty-seven degrees Fahrenheit to fifty-one degrees. Obviously, it would take considerably less energy to maintain a house at seventy degrees Fahrenheit when it's nestled into forty-seven degree earth than when it's being blasted by minus-thirty degree winds.

In many areas of the country, soil temperatures at their minimum and maximum temperature ranges are nearly three months behind those on the surface. It takes a long, hot summer to warm the earth three degrees. By autumn, when other people are beginning to use their furnaces, however, the earth is warmer than the outside air. Conversely, the earth drops to its lowest level as the heat of the summer nears.

As a matter of fact, your city's water department takes the earth's constant temperature into account when it installs water mains. If you've ever wondered how you can have cold running water when the outdoor temperature's wind chill factor is minus forty-five degrees, you may now understand why the water isn't frozen. The city's water mains are under the frost level of the ground, where the earth is warmer than thirty-two degrees Fahrenheit.

The Ecology House

One of the most famous underground homes, architect John Barnard's Ecology House, saves about sixty percent of the fuel use and cost necessary to maintain a similar home above ground. To allow the sun to penetrate every windowed room in the house, the Ecology House has a three-hundred-square-foot atrium at its south end. Walls are poured concrete reinforced with steel rods. The roof is composed of eight-inch thick precast concrete panels, covered with twelve to eighteen inches of earth. Styrene foam insulation—two inches thick on the side walls and roof and one inch thick under the floor slab—was applied to the exterior surfaces of the home.

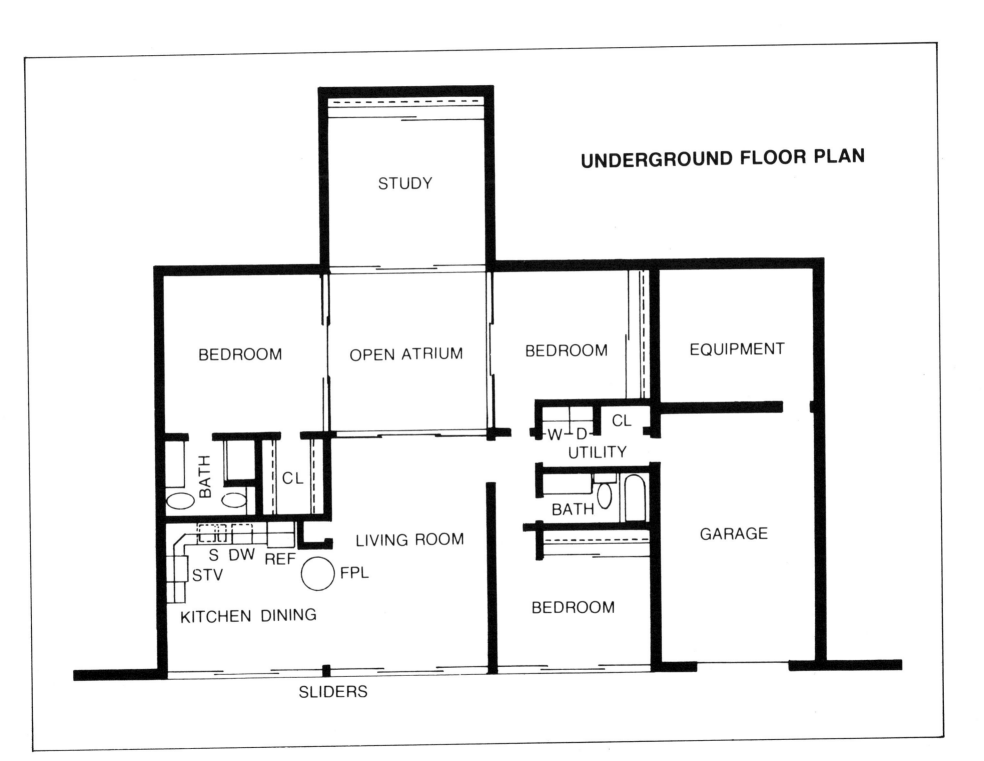

UNDERGROUND FLOOR PLAN

STUDY

BEDROOM

OPEN ATRIUM

BEDROOM

EQUIPMENT

CL

W D

UTILITY

BATH

CL

BATH

GARAGE

LIVING ROOM

S DW REF

STV

FPL

KITCHEN DINING

BEDROOM

SLIDERS

The Atlantic Beach Dune-
houses designed by William
Morgan, A.I.A. are set into
a 15-foot high duneside over-
looking the ocean.

Courtesy of William Morgan,
A.I.A. Photo by Creative
Photographic Service

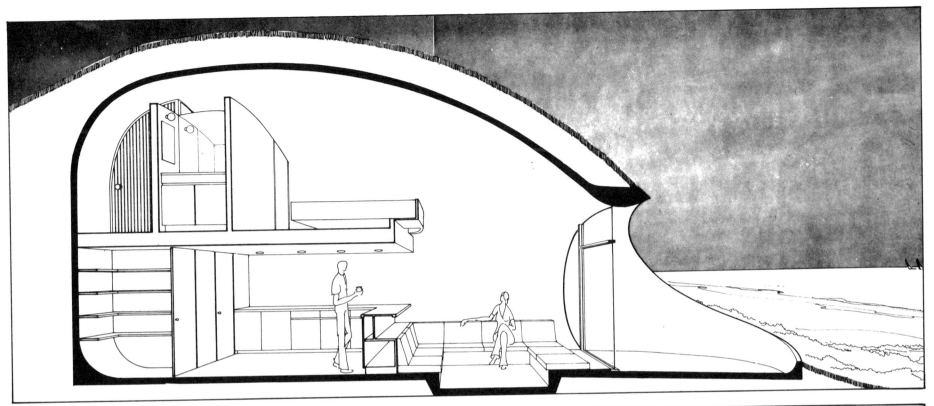

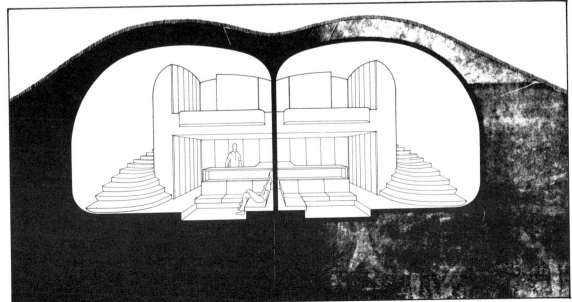

This page and overleaf:

Presentation drawings for
William Morgan's Atlantic
Beach, Florida, dunehouses.
Courtesy of William Morgan,
A.I.A.

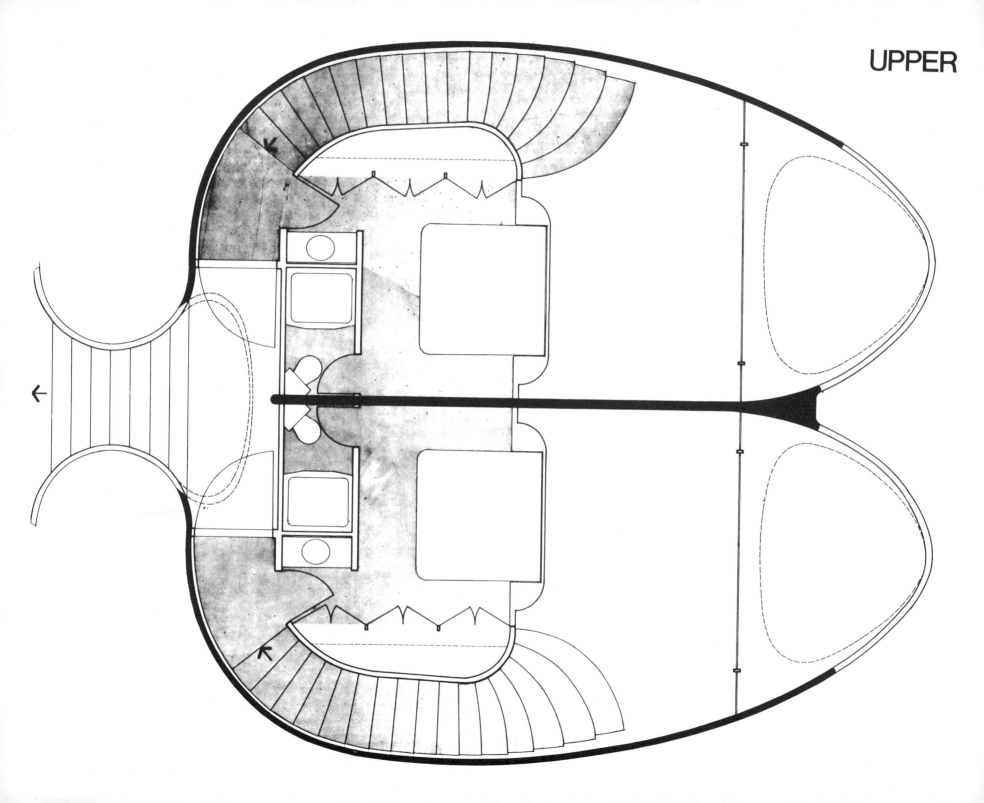

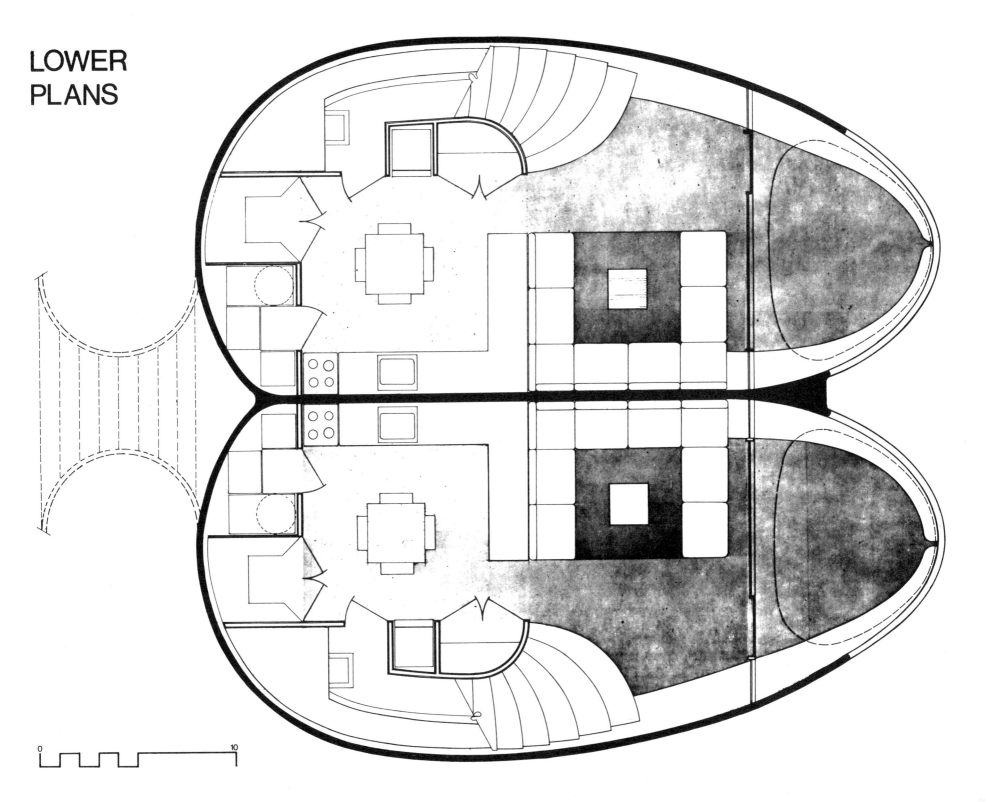

LOWER
PLANS

0　　　　　　　　　10

Underground Housing— Returning to Our Roots

UNDERGROUND FLOOR PLAN

Designed by architect John Barnard, Jr., A.I.A., this underground house features windows in every major room of the house.
Drawing by Ken Nash

Facing page:
Although underground housing is still in the experimental stages, its primary attraction seems to stem from the homes' inherent energy savings. This house was designed by John Barnard, Jr., A.I.A.

The flooring of the Ecology House is poured concrete. Heating ducts and electrical conduits are buried in the ground. Waterproofing of the Ecology House consists of three plies of asbestos felt and hot pitch on the roof, and hot pitch alone on the side walls.

Construction of the Ecology House began after the site was excavated to accommodate the entire building. Footings for the floor slab and the walls were cast in concrete at the site. To support the precast concrete roof, steel beams and columns were installed. Curb beams of concrete and stairs to the atrium level were cast. Finally, the entire structure was waterproofed and insulated, and the earth was backfilled.

To minimize the danger of leaks in the home, the Ecology House has no openings through the roof slab. Chimney, air intake and exhaust ducts, plumbing vents and so on all pass through the side walls. A standard home air conditioning unit not only provides the usual cooling, but also handles ventilation, humidification and dehumidification; it also contains an electrostatic air filter to reduce static electricity in the home.

Because construction is relatively simple, Barnard says most of the labor behind an underground house can be supplied by unskilled workers. However, if you are building an underground house, you will need a contractor to pour the concrete and to make sure the insulation and waterproofing are correctly completed. Even so, construction costs of approximately $27 per square foot are about seventy-five percent of the cost of a more conventionally constructed home.

In underground housing, drainage is paramount in importance and must be carefully designed into the structure. In the Ecology House, natural drainage through the atrium floor is more than adequate to handle the heaviest rainfall in Massachusetts. But if the house were built in a location where the water doesn't naturally drain through the atrium floor, the land would have to be gravity-drained, via a vertical pipe, for instance, to a lower point on the site. Otherwise

you would be wading through the ultimate mud puddle whenever it rained.

Obviously, you would not want to build an underground house in either swampy or solid rock areas. While you could probably blast out a big enough hole in solid rock to place your home, you wouldn't be able to fill in the spaces around the house with rock when it was completed. In swamp land, on the other hand, you wouldn't be able to keep the site excavated long enough to let the concrete dry thoroughly before you filled the earth back around the home.

Before you consider building an underground home, check with your architect. He or she will be familiar with the site's soil and other conditions. Your architect also may help you in financing the home. Lenders are cautious investors. If you cannot prove to them that the house will work, they aren't going to lend you the money to build it. The architect's plans may help convince a doubtful lender that you aren't wild-eyed and ready to foam at the mouth just because you want to build your home underground.

Most homes built today require minimal upkeep for the first ten to fifteen years. After twenty years, however, a wood-frame building—and most homes built in this country feature wood-frame construction even if they have brick or stone facades—often needs a considerable amount of exterior maintenance. Gutters need to be replaced. Termite damage may need to be repaired. The exterior probably will need repainting and reputtying, since materials are constantly subjected to rain and snow.

If you are forty-five now and you're planning to build your own home, you can count on that home needing high-cost repairs just when you are ready to retire and live on a decreased income. By omitting perishable materials, underground homes avoid this type of deterioration. Instead, they are constructed of glass, concrete and anodized aluminum, which are not as easily eroded as conventional home materials. If the home features fire-safe construction, fire insur-

ance coverage may also be lowered. You do not have to concern yourself with termite damage, since even the mightiest termite will turn up his nose at concrete for lunch.

Underground and Solar

In New Canaan, Connecticut, architect Land Gores and heating consultant Paul Sturges constructed an energy-saving house that is partially underground. The house is practically a laboratory of heat conservation techniques. It features three different systems to provide its heating needs—solar collectors, a heat exchange system using underground pipes that tap heat stored in the earth, and a second heat exchange system that employs fireplace heat.

Apart from twenty-one square feet of solar collectors on the southern part of the 4,000-square-foot home's roof, the house doesn't appear to be unconventional. The lower level, containing four bedrooms, is underground. Through sliding glass doors, each bedroom opens onto a small, sunken courtyard with a removable translucent roof. If the removable roof sounds like a hassle, keep in mind that the roof is at ground level, eliminating the need for ladders and superhuman balance. This openness helps to relieve the sensation of being trapped underground, and permits the courtyard to serve as a greenhouse for plants.

Since underground dampness can be a problem, the house's foundation walls must be kept dry for maximum heat conservation. So Sturges and Gores placed a layer of corrugated metal, similar to flashing, about a foot beneath the surface of the ground and extending ten feet from the perimeter of the house. The metal acts as an underground canopy, preventing water from soaking into the ground near the house.

The heart of the project's heating and cooling system is a pipe, two feet in diameter, that loops around the house more than eight feet underground. Because the earth's temperature varies little from day to day below the frost line, the house uses the heat stored in the surrounding

earth for part of its heating needs. (In the New Canaan area, the temperature of the earth below the frost line remains constant at fifty-two degrees Fahrenheit.)

In the winter, cool air is pumped out of the house through the pipe, which warms the air. As the heated air returns to the house, a heat exchanger is employed. The heat exchanger uses a collection of pipes filled with freon, the refrigerant often used in air conditioners. The air loses its heat to the freon and is blown back out into the underground pipe. Meanwhile, the heated freon is pumped into a compressor that raises its temperature to about 220 degrees. Then the freon travels through two more heat exchangers to heat the hot water supply for the home and to warm the air in the living spaces.

In the summertime, the process is reversed. The air in the underground pipe is cooled by the earth and used to precool the freon. Even though the temperature change achieved by this underground method is not great, it does reduce the house's dependence on fossil fuels. However, this system does rely on electricity to power the fans, pumps and compressors and to operate the house's lights, refrigeration and well pump.

Carrying the heat exchanger concept further, Sturges installed what he calls a Thriftexchanger for the home's fireplaces. Most fireplaces can lose up to ninety percent of the heat up the chimney. Sturges' solution was to close the fireplace's flue damper and place glass in front of the fireplace, turning the fireplace into a kiln that produces very high-temperature heat. This heated air is channeled into the Thriftexchanger. Patented and designed by Sturges, the Thriftexchanger is a collection of pipes and ducts that multiplies the heat being produced. Then this heat is circulated through the house by a duct system in the walls. The Thriftexchanger is also tied to the hot water system. When in use, the Thriftexchanger can heat approximately twenty gallons of water an hour.

No one seems to know exactly how much

Right:
According to architect John Barnard, Jr., A.I.A., you can save energy underground and still have floor to ceiling windows.

Left:
Underground homes feature the ultimate in privacy designed by John Barnard, Jr., A.I.A.

Underground Housing— Returning to Our Roots

energy can be saved by underground housing, but in studies done at minus twenty-five degrees Fahrenheit, Dr. Bligh discovered that heat loss through a wall filled with eight inches of insulation is 6.5 times greater than that through an uninsulated, underground concrete wall.

Architect John Barnard suggests that his energy-saving underground design can reduce heating needs by sixty percent. Dr. Bligh maintains that savings as high as seventy-five percent are possible. At Arizona State, James Scalise of the College of Architecture claims that a thin layer of soil on the roof of a house, along with the earth berm around it, can reduce energy usage by thirty percent. Whatever the statistics, solar heating becomes very practical for underground houses, where heating needs are cut by at least half, because the solar system can be proportionately reduced.

Barnard estimates that the underground houses he designs cost approximately twenty-five percent less to build than do comparable, above-grade frame houses. Other architects, such as Malcolm Wells of Cherry Hill, New Jersey, and William Morgan of Jacksonville, Florida, say underground houses may cost five to ten percent more than traditional housing, at least initially. The experts do agree that underground houses, when they begin to be mass-produced, will be substantially cheaper than those of standard construction.

Although the actual construction of an underground home isn't particularly complicated, there are a few drawbacks. No one knows precisely how much heating or cooling, if any, is needed. To determine the heating and cooling requirements of a conventional house, the builder consults the standards published by the American Society of Heating, Refrigeration and Air-Conditioning Engineers (ASHRAE). These specifications don't apply to earth-covered buildings, since heat loss depends not only on the heat flow properties of the building materials, but also on the heat conductivity of the soil. Deep, com-

pacted soil conducts heat much more easily than loose, dry soil. Currently, only a detailed soil analysis of each building site can tell the architect and the contractor what to expect.

In 1978, Dr. Bligh and his colleagues at the University of Minnesota were trying to remedy this situation. They had a $242,000 grant from the National Science Foundation to study an underground building constructed on the Minnesota campus. To validate the study for most of the country, they used five different types of soil as backfill. Then they developed a computer program based on the data collected on the underground building. Very shortly, ASHRAE standards may be written based on their findings.

Weight also can be a problem in underground housing. The roofs are covered with six inches to four feet of earth. Building codes require conventional roofs to support between thirty and forty pounds of weight per square foot. In northern climates, snow loads also are added to the roofing specifications. Since an underground house is supporting packed earth, it will need a very strong roofing system.

Unlike conventional housing, insulation in underground houses must be installed on the outside of the structure. That means that careful waterproofing is essential, in order to prevent leaks. You also have to pay particular attention to the water table in your area of the country. If it's only ten feet below the top layer of ground, you won't be able to build your home underground without a great many headaches and expensive site work. Check with your architect on local conditions.

In addition, once you build your home underground, you cannot easily add another bedroom or family den. You'll want to incorporate every possible space into the initial design. If you can get financing, almost any building site (except swampland and hard rock) is adaptable to underground construction. If you want to come out on top of the energy spiral, you may need to go underground.

Chapter 7
Recycling—Trend of the 1980s

Facing page:
This elaborate home in Southern Wisconsin is really a barn. Architect: Stanley Tigerman, A.I.A.

Pointing to the increasing cost of replacing anything, most housing industry experts concur that recycling will dominate the 1980s. This, of course, is especially applicable to new homes. An average new house costs nearly $50,000, placing it out of reach of the average breadwinner's $15,000 annual income, so families are looking for ways to remodel already existing homes.

Older buildings, once scoffed at by many home buyers, are beginning to look more attractive. Older buildings are becoming too valuable to tear down. However, remodeling can be costly. One prominent building contractor estimates that remodeling costs for older homes range between thirty and fifty percent of the cost of building new housing. Building codes are one reason for this discrimination. In Massachusetts, for instance, if the remodeling costs exceed a quarter of the assessed value of the building, the whole building must be brought up to the state's current codes. A $5,000 remodeling job can skyrocket to $25,000.

Nevertheless, rehabilitating older homes is becoming more popular because of the high cost of new housing and its resultant increase in mortgages. The National Home Improvement Council, Inc., estimates that approximately forty-five million single-family homes in the U.S. are twenty or more years old. For a house, twenty years is a critical age. By that time, equipment has begun to sputter and fail. The 1958 house is also underinsulated by today's energy-conscious standards. Home owners know all too well that a poorly insulated house costs them hard-earned money in their increased power bills. Style and technology have also changed. Today's home buyer wants more modern kitchens and bathrooms than those normally found in older homes.

To some extent, legislation will spur remodeling. Long-discussed federal tax incentives are likely to become law very shortly. At least two states have passed temporary tax abatements for the newly remodeled house.

In addition to offering architectural styles that are rarely duplicated today, older homes may have been constructed better and frequently may cost less than new housing. Generally, an older home can be bought for considerably less than the $50,000 needed for a new home, and it may give you more living space for your money. Many of the homes built in the 1920s and 1930s are testimonials to quality craftmanship. Spacious rooms, bay windows and natural woodwork add charm and rich personality to these homes.

Older homes don't hide their flaws as easily as modern houses do. Cracked plaster and missing bathroom tiles are hard to miss. With some investigation, it's easy to determine the overall condition of the house. The hidden components of the house—the electrical, plumbing and heating systems—probably are outdated. You should have a home inspector or other professional inspect the home thoroughly before you buy. You also would be wise to have a professional examine the condition of the roof and the foundation. Ask him or her to check for signs of termite damage.

If your architect or home inspector finds structural problems in the house, you may be able to negotiate a lower price. Make sure the repair costs will not exceed the money you save by purchasing an older home. Before you sign anything, get cost estimates to determine renovation expenses. Most professional remodelers suggest that you add the cost estimates for the repairs, plus ten to fifteen percent, to the asking price of the house. If your total is near or below the going rate for houses in the neighborhood, you probably have found a good buy.

Before you buy a house, you may want to do some detective work on your own. Remember, neighbors who tell you they got the price they wanted aren't really telling you anything. However, there is a reliable source in most areas of the country. Generally, the exact amount a house sold for is a matter of public record to be found with a little clever digging at the country recorder's office.

Facing page:
If you like natural wood, barn interiors can offer you knotty pine.
Architect: Stanley Tigerman, A.I.A.

Creative use of windows and exterior refinishing can give you a beautiful barn home.
Architect: Stanley Tigerman, A.I.A.

First, get a legal description of the property you are thinking of buying. For a marginal fee, often less than a dollar, you can get that information from a clerk in the city's map department. If your city doesn't have a map department, check the legal description in the county treasurer's office. Once you have the legal description, take it to the recorder of deeds. A clerk there will help you find the recording number in the proper tract book.

Take the recording number to the proper location—ask the clerk—in your county building, where all transactions generally are kept on microfilm. The clerk in this department will pull the correct microfilm card from the files and direct you to a microfilm machine. Since you will find more than one deed recorded on the microfilm card, run down the other ones until you locate one that matches the recording number. Then note the value of the revenue stamp attached to the document. Each dollar of stamp value represents $1,000 of the contract price. So, if the stamp on the lot you're looking at is valued at $45, you know the property sold for $45,000.

Property owners often can request that the stamps be removed from the document before it is microfilmed. In the case of home sales, this occurs about five percent of the time. If you're a buyer, learning the price of a comparable house will give you an idea of whether the asking price is in line. You can also find out how much the seller paid for the house he's selling by following the same process.

You can count on an old-fashioned, outdated kitchen and antiquated bathrooms when you buy an older home. These two areas frequently need to be remodeled. You should consider their costs and get bids on those remodeling jobs before you buy the home.

Your utility bills for an older home also will be higher. You'll probably want to install more insulation to make the home energy efficient. To find out just how much work needs to be done, ask to see the owner's utility bills for the past year.

Lenders tend to be shy of mortgages on older homes. They may require larger downpayments—sometimes twenty-five to forty percent—on older homes. Depending on the neighborhood and the condition of the house, the lender also may hesitate to grant you a loan. Remember, the lender is out to make money, not to lose it. Most lenders learned the following rules in their first appraisal course: neighborhoods are built; they stabilize; they decay. So no rational loan officer wants to put long-term money in an area that is either in the stable or in the down cycle.

Savings and loan institutions are unsure of recycling and are not likely to change their attitude overnight. Customers and builders must re-educate them with solid proposals that show how the job of remodeling or rehabilitating means cents and sense. As the lenders learn more about recycling and become involved in several successful recycling jobs, they will be less likely to give higher interest rates on older-home mortgages.

Location of the recycling project is very important to the lender. You may be able to get an eighty-percent, thirty-year loan for a house in an improving community, but only sixty percent on a fifteen-year loan for a similar home in a marginal or changing neighborhood. Often referred to as redlining, this habit of lenders is slowly being broken.

As interest in revitalizing old neighborhoods grows, communities are developing programs that encourage lenders to invest in these areas. In fact, some suburbs near metropolitan areas have even made official commitments to halt or reverse decline in their cities. Cleveland Heights, for instance, is a seventy-year-old city on the eastern border of Cleveland. In that area, the city fathers established a housing agency. The agency was to promote and preserve Cleveland Heights by developing programs along with community organizations. Lenders in the area worked with minority and youth groups as well as with senior citizens and religious, business,

This is the only one of many Victorian homes in the San Francisco area restored by San Francisco Victoriana.
Photo: California Redwood Association

One Victorian home expert estimates that each dollar spent in restoration increases the home's value by three dollars.
Photo: California Redwood Association

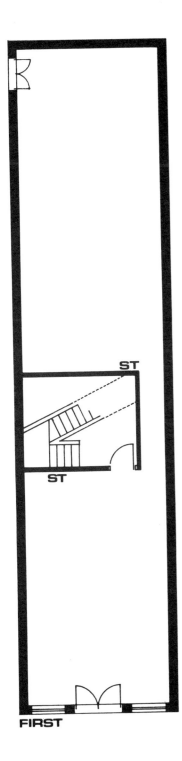

FIRST

ST

ST

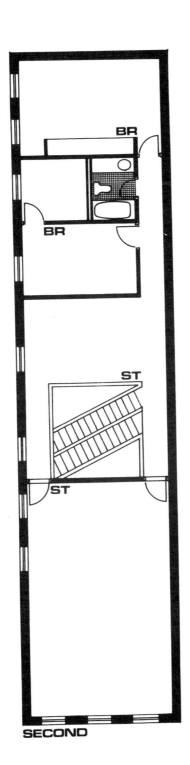

BR

BR

ST

ST

SECOND

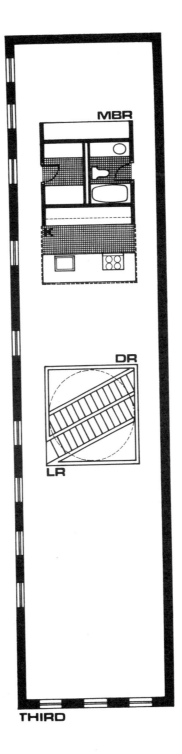

MBR

K

DR

LR

THIRD

GINZEL
STUDIO 1969
BOOTH
& NAGLE
ARCHITECTS
CHICAGO
0   4'   8'

Since the cooks in the Ginzel Studio home—in a remodeled bakery building—are extroverted, they like the open kitchen-dining-living space on the top level of the building. The wide central stairway leads down to bedrooms at the second level and ground-floor studios.
Photos by Jonas Dovydenas. Architects: Booth, Nagle, and Hartray, Ltd.

The exterior of this 22-foot wide, four story townhouse has been restored. Note that new casement windows and a stairway to the first floor entry were installed. Another stairway was also installed at the rear.
Photographer: Arthur LaZar.
Architects: Booth, Nagle, and Hartray, Ltd.

academic and government leaders. Pulling together, the community was able to find several ways to make mortgages available to home buyers who wanted to purchase and rehabilitate older homes in the community. Young couples can buy post-World War I frame houses for $25,000 to $30,000. While the houses do need work, they are available to first-time buyers who otherwise would not be able to buy at all.

Cleveland Heights isn't the only city doing this type of recycling. In some Boston suburbs, old Victorian and Colonial homes are selling in the $28,000 to $45,000 range. Older neighborhoods in the Chicago area also offer home buying possibilities. Homes in these neighborhoods frequently range from $18,000 to $40,000. The price for new homes in the Chicago area now averages $57,500—so the savings can be a real bargain.

The suburbs aren't the only places to look for houses that can be remodeled. A number of young, first-time buyers also are finding terrific buys in sprawling old houses or row houses in the heart of the inner city. Sometimes these homes are called townhouses or brownstones, and they can offer a fine alternative in housing, even though you'll need to do a great deal of work.

Sensing the need to save the inner cities, modern-day pioneers are even rebuilding entire communities and neighborhoods. In Chicago, for example, the local citizenry in Logan Square banded together to save a neighborhood that was being taken over by street gangs. To gain support for their revitalizing projects, neighborhood associations affiliated with local churches and other civic groups were started.

One of their major hurdles is still redlining, a practice whereby lenders refuse mortgage loans in areas they consider questionable. The term comes from the red lines that lenders literally draw around sections of city maps, indicating areas where they think it is risky to invest money. Although redlining is still being done, there are laws to prohibit it. The Secretary of the U.S. Department of Housing and Urban De-

velopment has urged lenders to allocate money that will increase the remodeling and revitalizing of these inner-city cores.

Unfortunately, de-slumming continues to be a struggle. In addition to fighting for mortgages, residents often need to become political activists, fighting city officials who want to raze the whole neighborhood and erect government projects. A perfectly charming neighborhood that needs a facelift can become the site of a cross-town expressway.

To maintain neighborhoods for both lower-income citizens and upper-middle class professionals is a constant fight. In Baltimore, Maryland, the Stirling Street Neighbors program is saving row houses built in the early 1800s. Originally, these homes were going to be demolished and replaced with low-income housing. However, a state senator recognized the historical significance of the neighborhood and worked to save the area. After several years of wheeling and dealing, the city fathers agreed that the area could be rehabilitated.

The city housing department started a homesteading program that sold each house for one dollar. Through the federal government, officials arranged for low-interest rehabilitation loans of approximately $15,000 for each homesteader. Under the plan, the homesteader received the deed for a dollar in return for his or her agreement to renovate the house within one year and to live there for three years. Today, forty-two homes have been restored.

Row houses can offer both charm and economy. Since the houses are attached, heating bills can be less and the owners can save on the cost of the land and insulation. If you plan to purchase a row house, you should check the soundproofing of the walls that you share with your neighbors. You also might want to see how private your backyard will be.

Local and federal government programs often support the regrowth of older neighborhoods. The HUD urban homesteading program is be-

thousand kilowatts. A megawatt is about 1,300 horsepower. (A Fiat engine, in comparison, probably produces about 85 horsepower.)

Methane digester is an insulated, air-tight container that augments the breakdown of organic wastes to produce methane gas, which is proving to be a useful bio fuel.

Photolysis is the chemical decomposition caused by radiation. For instance, solar energy can break water into hydrogen and oxygen.

Photovoltaic relates to the electricity produced by the action of solar radiation on a solar cell or battery.

Pyronometer is a device that measures solar radiation.

Pyroheliometer is an even more accurate instrument for measuring solar radiation.

Rock storage is a bin or basement filled with rock acting as a heat reservoir for a solar energy system. For each square foot of solar collectors, about fifty pounds of rock are needed to store the heat.

Selective surface is a special coating applied to solar flat-plate collectors. The surface absorbs most of the incoming solar energy.

Solar cell, or solar battery, is a device, frequently made of silicon, that converts sunlight directly into energy.

Solar constant is the average amount of solar radiation that reaches the earth's atmosphere each minute. The solar constant is two langleys, or two gram-calories per square centimeter.

Solar cooker is an oven or reflector that cooks with solar heat.

Solar furnace is a device that employs mirror reflectors or lenses to produce extremely high heat.

Solar pump is a device that uses solar energy to run a motor that pumps water.

Solar still is equipment that uses the sun's heat to desalt water.

Solarimeter is a simple solar radiation measuring instrument that uses solar cells.

Sun tracking is following the sun with a solar collector, thus making the collector more effective.

Thermosyphoning is the principle by which water circulates automatically between a flat-plate collector and a storage tank, gradually increasing the water's temperature.

Trickling water collector is a solar collector featuring water which is pumped to the top of a roof and then trickles down valleys of collectors, amassing heat along the way.

"Venetian blind" collector features a venetian blind that is painted flat black on one side and placed between two panes of glass. When closed (with the black side to the sun) it collects heat that is transferred to air circulated between the glass panes.

Kitchen at the rear of the first floor.

The interior of this townhouse was nearly gutted. Very little of the plumbing or heating could be saved. The sculptural stairway shown here creates a vertical shaft, connecting floors.
Photographer: Arthur LaZar.
Architects: Booth, Nagle, and Hartray, Ltd.

Above and facing page:
In Chicago, this North Astor Home is a three and a half story, orange brick and limestone residence designed in a Georgian Revival Style. The second floor has a continuous cornice that wraps around the home. Notice also the round window bays.
Photos by Ralph Youngren.
Architects: Metz, Train, Olson, and Youngren.

coming a model for many inner city rehabilitation projects across the nation. In the HUD program, the buyer pays $1 for a repossessed house whose owners defaulted on a government-backed mortgage loan. The homesteader must bring the house up to the current building code standards within eighteen months and live in the home for at least three years.

In 1975, HUD began the homesteading program in twenty-three demonstration cities, both large and small. Chicago, New York and Boston offer the program, as does Decatur, Georgia (population 22,000).

A number of other projects offer assistance to buyers interested in homesteading. The National Association of Realtors has a *Project Pride* program. Under this program, local boards of realtors buy older, decaying homes and sell them on a nonprofit basis, to reverse the decline of a neighborhood.

The Urban Reinvestment Task Force is a joint effort between the federal financial regulatory agencies and HUD. The task force has helped establish nonprofit *Neighborhood Housing Services* (NHS) in forty cities, including Dallas, Pittsburgh and Cincinnati.

NHS brings together residents, local citizens groups, government officials and lenders to assure total community participation. This team cooperates to overcome redlining and other discriminatory practices. While they make money available to homesteaders, they also help existing homeowners refurbish their homes. NHS provides rehabilitation counseling as well as construction monitoring on the homeowner's project. The staff will also work with lenders to help arrange loans for residents. To obtain further information on this program, contact the Urban Reinvestment Task Force, 1120 Nineteenth Street, N.W., Suite 600, Washington, D.C. 20036.

Getting the Work Done
If you plan to buy a home and remodel it, you must find a contractor who will redo the bathroom and build a new kitchen. If you know exactly what you want done, you may not wish to hire an architect or designer. But how do you find a competent remodeling contractor whose fees are reasonable? One source you may wish to check is the National Home Improvement Council, Inc. Homebuilding contractors comprise most of the council's membership. (A listing of regional offices and the main office is on page 150.) Most architects also will supply you with a list of the contractors they rely on.

Word of mouth is the best recommendation. Contractors base their breadwinning on satisfied customers. After you have narrowed the list in the Yellow Pages to three or four well qualified contractors, you can check them further through your local consumer council and the Better Business Bureau. Both agencies keep active complaint and litigation records, run credit checks and verify the contractor's reliability. In some communities, the local consumer council even licenses home-improvement contractors. Since licensing varies from city to city, you should ask for thorough explanations of your local regulations, insurance requirements and pertinent details.

To avoid misunderstandings that might end up in court, make sure everything is put in writing. As you check your contractor list, compose a detailed description of exactly what work needs to be done. For instance, you may need rough floor plans and details of walls and ceilings that show the exact placement of electrical outlets, switches, lights, shelves, closets, counters, sinks, tubs, doors, windows, etc. Measurements, or at least approximations of each, should be prepared.

To protect your interests, specify brand names, manufacturers' model numbers and color codes for all appliances and fixtures. This will tell you what is available and how much it costs. When you can, you should also list the brand names and grades for the building materials, such as paint, wood finishes, flooring, windows, walls,

The Illinois Corn Crib weekend retreat, designed by Cynthia Weese of Weese, Seegers, Hickey, and Weese Architects Ltd., had so much character that the owners wanted to retain its exterior look. The building had a central drive, with storage bins on both sides and on the top. In the renovation, utilities were brought in through the drive. It was filled in with a conversation area on one side, and a utility core on the other. The grain bins on the top became sleeping rooms.

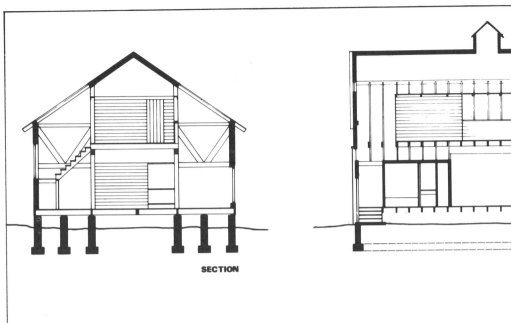

SECTION

SECTION

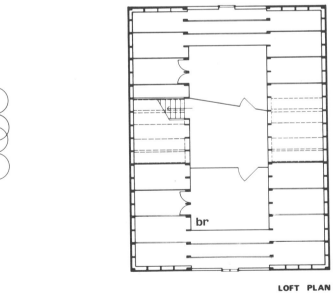

lr

FIRST FLOOR PLAN

br

LOFT PLAN

ICC

Recycling—
Trend of the 1980s

Above and facing page:
Two 18th-century frame houses and an early 19th-century barn were moved from various sites along a busy Long Island highway and relocated on a 40-acre oceanfront property. Architect Howard Barnstone painstakingly restored the buildings with original or hand-hewn lumber, plaster, milk paint, special hand-cut shingles, and original 18th-century hardwares.
Photos by Bill Maris, courtesy of the American Institute of Architects.

doors, roofing, siding, etc.

Unless the plans are specified carefully, the contractor will follow his or her personal instincts in construction. If you want to install cabinets or closets, you probably should take measurements of others in the house so that you know how large you really want that closet. Will you be storing brooms in it or your full wardrobe? Exact dimensions will allow the contractor to build just what you want.

You also should become familiar with building materials and the equipment offered in catalogs, home improvement centers and lumberyards. You can also contact the local building department for information. Its inspectors can supply you with the exact legal specifications for any project.

As each contractor comes to make estimates, you can also tap his or her knowledge. You should have the contractor outline every step of the construction process and list all the materials necessary for the job. The contractor might suggest an alternative you didn't think was possible.

You should provide each contractor with a copy of your detailed project description. Be sure to request that bids specify every detail of the project as well as the total cost and the completion date. When you have all these pieces of information, you will be able to compare the bids, and you will know that the contractor isn't substituting materials you haven't chosen.

When you review the bids, a good rule of thumb is to throw out the highest and the lowest ones first. Often, you will find the ones in the middle are more accurate parameters of what the job will cost. The highest bidder may be too busy. And, while the lowest bid does not necessarily mean the work will be shoddy, it may suggest that the contractor is short on work and desperate to cover overhead expenses.

After you locate a suitable contractor, ask him or her for a reasonable estimate and completion date for the work. Ask the contractor to supply you with a list of customers who have had similar work done on their homes. If you visit a couple of the contractor's clients, you will be able to see the quality of the contractor's workmanship, and the clients might be willing to share some hindsight with you.

If you are having any major renovation done on your home, you'll need the advice of a lawyer to write the contract. If your personal lawyer isn't versed in construction terminology, he or she will be able to recommend an attorney who is. Don't use the contractor's lawyer—that places the lawyer in a potentially conflicting position.

Whether or not you use a lawyer, the contract must include the entire project description and all the materials and plans needed to complete the project. It also must include the names and license numbers of all subcontractors and the homeowner's right to substitute another subcontractor if the one named provides poor workmanship.

The contract also must declare a specific completion date, followed by the phrase, "Time of the essence." The contractor may not agree to the date you propose, and you may have to compromise. But get a *specific* date. That date allows the homeowner to minimize lost time without being liable for breach of contract.

You should always include the phrase, "workmanship must be the best known in the trade." It sounds like legal jargon, but it is important. The contract also should contain a guaranteed maximum price for the completed job and a schedule of payments. On minor projects, the total price often is broken into three payments—one as a downpayment, the second due when the work is well underway and the third due when the job is completed.

Of the one-third downpayment, you should pay ten percent on signing the contract. The other twenty-three percent should be paid when the contractor's crew reports for work. As in larger projects, the middle payment should be made after the contractor presents you with paid bills for labor and materials.

Recycling—
Trend of the 1980s

Left:
This Victorian townhouse, 15 feet wide and three stories high, was repaired and restored to its original character.

Right:
The center of the house is opened to a skylight above the stairway.
Photographer: Arthur LaZar.
Architects: Booth, Nagle, and Hartray, Ltd.

Left:
Row homes like these on
Chicago's near north side can
be found in most major cities.
Often they feature beautiful
bay windows and high ceilings
as well as detailed exteriors
and plenty of woodworking
details inside.
Photos: Rita Tatum.

Right:
Older homes in the heart of
major cities across the country are being saved.
Photo: Rita Tatum.

On large remodeling jobs, you should try to negotiate the lowest downpayment possible and reserve a percentage of the total cost—the higher the better—for your final payment. While the job is in progress, you should make payments only after you have received paid bills for materials and labor from the contractor.

The contract should also require the contractor to secure all the necessary building permits. It should stipulate that the electrical systems be inspected by the National Board of Fire Underwriters. And it will need the clause, "Final payment will be withheld until the contractor presents releases or proof of payment from major suppliers and all subcontractors." Finally, remember that the bottom line of the contract says, "No agreements unless recorded above are binding." Everything you want done must be spelled out clearly.

Even if you have a tight contract and a reputable contractor, you should count on supervising the project to some extent. Architects spend hours checking the work to make sure it is going according to plans and specifications. Since each project can run into potential problems, you will be called on to make practical and esthetic decisions during the work. During critical stages, you should be available to stop by the site, in case some problem comes up that needs your input. Otherwise, you might come home from work to discover that the door to your kitchen opens inward and bangs right into the refrigerator. If any changes have to be made, they should be executed before the final touches are in place.

During the construction, you may find yourself tearing out your hair. But remember that if you have done your homework, chances are you are going to be pleased with the results.

Right and facing page:
Designed by Myron
Goldfinger, A.I.A., this New
York home restoration is re-
strained and modest on the
exterior, which contrasts
nicely with the detailed interiors.
Photos by Norman McGrath,
Courtesy of the American Institute of Architects.

Chapter 8

Group Living: Condominiums, Co-operatives and City Lofts

Facing page:
The Carlyle in Chicago, located along the famous Lake Shore Drive, is one of the most prestigious addresses in the city. The elegant high-rise caters to prominent Chicagoans who want a home in the heart of the city.
Photo: Rita Tatum.

In the face of soaring home costs and widespread land shortages, young Americans are finding it nearly impossible to buy a stick-built house just like the one Mom and Dad have. So they are looking more creatively at alternative housing arrangements. Today's tie-and-briefcase set is discovering that the communal living espoused by the placard-carrying protestors of the 1960s does have its merits.

Slightly reminiscent of college dorm life, these modern dwellings are cropping up all over the country in the form of group houses, co-operatives and condominiums. You will find most of them in the trendy, high-rent, high-divorce-rate cities—New York, Philadelphia, San Francisco, Chicago, Los Angeles, Minneapolis, Washington, D.C. and others. As the trend takes hold, however, even senior citizens and middle-aged buyers are getting in on co-operative living. These housing developments are spreading from the cities out into the suburbs and beyond.

Once adopted only by bachelors and secretaries on tight budgets, this type of living experience now attracts government lawyers, scientists, legislative aides, economists and other professionals. Most group households, co-operatives and condominiums have no common interest or ideology other than basic compatibility. Economics is still the prime motivation in the group living trend. The average home is prohibitively expensive for young professionals, even though they may have quite respectable incomes.

Young professionals, who aren't as tied to one city and one job for the rest of their lives as their parents were, see definite advantages in group living which offers all kinds of assistance to working men and women who don't have the time or the energy to putter around the yard or fix the tiles in the bathroom. Some form of co-operative living also fills in social gaps for newcomers to big cities.

Land shortages, placing a crimp in conventional home buying, have caused lot prices to rise two to four times as fast as housing prices. According to the U.S. Housing Markets Survey, Baltimore, Washington, D.C., Miami, Fort Lauderdale, Denver, Los Angeles, San Diego and San Francisco markets have lot shortages so severe that home building will be curtailed for years to come.

That may be one of the reasons that co-operative living is growing so quickly. According to Census Bureau estimates, approximately 204,000 Americans now live in co-ed arrangements with two or more unrelated adults. That's double the 1970 figure. No one has tallied the number of unisex arrangements, but companies that specialize in placing roommates say about half the groups are male or female only. That implies that at least 400,000 unrelated adults live together in groups larger than two persons.

Condominiums

In 1977, condominium production totaled 200,000 units. Of those, 100,000 were in new multi-unit buildings, and another 50,000 were in new single-family housing. The additional 50,000 were in conversions. Based on Census Bureau data, the survey concluded that absorption rates of new condominiums improved significantly in the last year. The survey reported that seventy-six percent of the multi-unit condominiums completed in the first half of 1977 were sold within three months! Census Bureau vacancy data indicated that as many as 75,000 units were sold last year from existing inventory. New and converted condominiums should total 300,000 by the end of 1978. All indications suggest the figure will continue to rise yearly.

The condominium revival comes largely from the return of favorable financing conditions and the choice by many young home buyers to return to the city, rather than opt for suburban living. Unwilling to conform to the new-car-in-the-driveway, new-child-on-the-way lifestyle of suburban living, these individuals usually want to be near their jobs and the cultural and entertainment possibilities offered inside the city, but they

don't have the money to buy posh brownstones. They're looking at new ways to protect themselves financially, without all the headaches normally associated with buying more traditional housing.

The U.S. Department of Housing and Urban Development estimates that within twenty years more than half of all Americans will live in some form of condominium or co-operative housing. Because the forms are so different, one of these housing alternatives may be right for you.

Basically a condominium is a form of ownership that allows the buyer to own a portion of a larger building, as well as an undivided share in the grounds and amenities surrounding the actual living unit. In other words, you receive two different types of property. First of all, you receive a deed, giving you ownership of the actual living space. But you also are a part owner of the property owned jointly by the condominium association. Shared by all owners of the condominium, this common property can include grounds, clubhouses, laundry facilities, sidewalks, etc.

Although you are spared the chores of mowing the lawn and pruning the dying Dutch elms, you do experience tax advantages, equity build-up and appreciation as owners of single-family homes do. If you would rather spend your time attending concerts or plotting your next move up the professional ladder than shoveling snow out of the driveway, a condominium may be just the housing alternative you need.

For some, the switch to owning is a spin-off from the very apartment they fell in love with two years ago, as more and more landlords convert massive apartment complexes into condominiums. If your building goes condominium, the advantages and the drawbacks will center primarily around your own unit. But if the building also contains commercial and retail space, you must consider a few other factors.

In some conversions, shops, offices and parking garages are separated from the residential space by the developer. He either retains control

of these spaces, or he sells them to other investors. In other set-ups, the condominium association owns the commercial and retail space. Those in the business of converting apartments into condominiums agree that no one arrangement is best. The type of building, the type of commercial space, the building's location and the developer all determine which system is best. To evaluate a prospective buy, know the alternatives for non-residential space. Remembering the following tips can help you make the best buy.

The biggest disadvantage of retaining the commercial and retail space is the management responsibility faced by the condominium association. In a converted building, the homeowners often are new to ownership or to living in multi-unit buildings. If the association owns the non-residential space, they must learn how to be landlords, as well as how to deal with the ins and outs of the property's residential section.

To set up the condominium association, all owner/members elect a board of directors to oversee the necessities of the complex. Condominium boards, unfortunately, often have high turnover rates, and this can cause problems for an association that owns the commercial space. As one budget consultant on converted projects said, "As a tenant, you may have no continuity of ownership. You might have a very good board to start with. But that could change quickly."

Nevertheless, the advantages in retaining control over the whole building complex do exist. They must be weighed against the disadvantages by any condominium buyer. As landlord, for instance, the association will have control over the type of tenant that occupies the leased space. Another plus is that the income from commercial and retail space can be substantial in some areas. This actually could result in lower monthly assessments for residential unit owners. Unlike the monthly maintenance fees, however, that income is taxable.

The condominium association generally hires out all maintenance chores. For instance, the

Living in the heart of a major city in row homes can be rewarding.
Photo: Rita Tatum.

Young families can find vibrant, older housing in the city. Although they may not have large front or back yards, these homes frequently are located close to public transportation and the cultural as well as entertaining attractions that larger cities afford.
Photos: Rita Tatum.

board hires firms to handle snow removal and garbage pickup, and also companies to maintain the common property or recreational facilities. Often the board of directors will hire a management firm to take charge of the daily operations of the total complex.

As an owner, you have one vote on any matter put before the association. If most members want a built-in swimming pool, they can have one—a mini-democracy in action. To support all the association's activities, you will pay a monthly fee.

Condominium complexes are as diverse as the individuals who live in them. They can be spanking new high-rises in the inner city, or sprawling, landscaped townhouses on the fringes of the metropolitan area. To meet the needs of today's buyer, numerous older in-town apartment buildings also are being converted into condominium complexes.

Naturally, shopping for a condominium involves as many details as shopping for a more conventional home. You shop around to find the best price as well as the type of condo that suits you.

Pay particular attention to the various neighborhoods, as well as to the residents of the complex. Are the current residents young families or primarily retired businessmen and their wives? Are they single? Do they *all* have Doberman pinschers that roam about looking for your Burmese cat? Ignoring such details can lead to a disappointing purchase. You probably will feel more comfortable if you choose a condo whose residents espouse similar lifestyles.

Once you've screened all the condominium candidates for the preliminaries—especially your pocketbook's limitations—revisit your key choices and find out a few more facts before you sign anything. Visit the manager and ask him or her to give you all the information he or she has on the condominium and the purchase transaction. Ask him or her any other questions you might have that the information doesn't cover. For instance, you may be concerned about park-

ing. Find out where garages are located and how much it will cost.

Before you sign a subscription or purchase agreement—or any other form of sales contract—read the declaration, bylaws, operating budget, management agreement and regulatory agreement (necessary if federal money is involved in the conversion). These documents tell you your rights and responsibilities as an owner of this particular piece of property. Occasionally these rules can be too restrictive to owners or too self-serving to the developers. As with any home purchase, it's a good idea to have your attorney study these documents and advise you on the purchase.

You may wish to interview some of the other owners in the buildings. Find out if they are satisfied with the building and its operation. If their attitude is negative, find out why they don't like the condominium.

You also may want to research the reputation of the management firm that operates the condo. If the firm's overall record is poor, you probably should rule this particular building out of the running. Once again, the residents of the building are good sources for such information.

Your local Better Business Bureau can advise you on the developer's and builder's reputations for workmanship. Are they known for quality construction? Check carefully for shoddy construction or signs of shortcuts taken in the building of the complex.

You need to know the total cost of the unit you're considering and what that purchase price includes. If the complex may be expanded, find out how that will affect you as a partial owner. Will it increase or decrease your payments?

Pay particular attention to the monthly amount you will be charged for upkeep of the grounds and for other amenities. At what rate will that amount increase in the future? Who makes those decisions? In some cases, the management firm can increase the costs.

How strong is the association you will be joining? How does it work? Does the association have the right of *first refusal* if you ever want to sell your property?

Can you arrange for financing? Do so before you give the manager a deposit. Financing is arranged in the same way as it is for a single-family dwelling. Many condos are financed conventionally, but you may be able to get FHA- or VA-backed financing on your own.

Will your deposit be refunded if the development fails or the terms of the agreement aren't met? If you're considering an older conversion, ask to see proof that the building meets current electrical, plumbing, fire and construction codes. If it doesn't, make sure that you won't have to share the costs in updating the building system.

Are the terms outlined in the purchase agreement? Do you understand the wording and the working of the agreement? It's in your best interest to have a lawyer check your agreement thoroughly for these points.

Will your downpayment money be used to help develop the rest of the complex? This may indicate a shaky situation. You may be asking for trouble without knowing it.

Ask to see a financial statement. Have your accountant or a lawyer interpret the figures for you. If the manager cannot offer you a financial statement, you should be wary of the complex.

Ask to see the liability insurance policy covering mishaps that may occur on the property. You will be responsible, of course, for such accidents as the friendly local bill collector falling on your marble floors, or any other such disaster that takes place in your own unit.

A further source of information is a free booklet from the U.S. Department of Housing and Urban Development. To obtain a copy of the 48-page book, *Questions About Condominiums,* send a postcard requesting it to the Consumer Information Center, Department 586E, Pueblo, Colorado 81009.

Co-operatives

Basically a form of free enterprise, co-operatives are non-profit corporations with shareholders, directors and officers. If you live in a co-operative you buy a share of stock in the nonprofit co-operative corporation. This gives you occupancy rights to a housing unit, as well as the tax advantages you would have with home ownership.

Several features distinguish co-operatives from any other form of housing in America today. First of all, co-op members jointly own the whole community, not just their individual homes. This allows them to protect their community against any changes they feel would be undesirable.

To protect the rights of all residents, members cooperate to hold down costs and to maintain quality standards. A sense of active participation causes low turnover, thereby creating a community where crime, vandalism and alienation are reduced or eliminated.

Although an estimated 1.4 million Americans now live in co-operative housing, co-operatives still are not a well-recognized form of housing. However, as single-family homes become less affordable and limited in availability, co-operatives become increasingly attractive.

If you decide to buy into a co-operative, you can choose from a variety of forms. Co-operatives are available as single-family homes, duplexes, townhouses, garden apartments, mid- and high-rise apartments and even mobile and modular homes.

Like condominiums, co-ops can be found throughout the U.S., but they are mostly located in or near major metropolitan areas. You will find them listed under co-operatives in the Yellow Pages of most telephone directories. Real estate ads in local papers also cover co-operatives. Your local U.S. Department or Housing and Urban Development offices of the local Board of Realtors can point out co-operatives in your area.

Another source of co-operative information is the National Association of Housing Co-operatives, 1828 L Street, N.W., Washington,

Basically a form of free enterprise, co-operatives are non-profit corporations with shareholders, directors and officers.
Photo: Rita Tatum.

99

Group Living: Condominiums, Co-operatives and City Lofts

D.C. 20036. In addition to supplying you with a *National Directory of Housing Co-operatives* for $5, the association can send you detailed information on the formation and operation of co-ops.

While a great number of co-operatives are federally subsidized to provide housing for low-income families and individuals, a sizable number also are financed conventionally. HUD-insured mortgages also are available. About 500 HUD-insured, unsubsidized co-ops with some 66,000 units exist in the U.S. today. Because it's often difficult to obtain financing for co-operatives, HUD insures mortgages for many of them.

People planning to move into a co-operative probably will be asked to sign a subscription agreement stating that if they are approved for membership by the co-op's board, they will pay a certain amount and pledge to become a resident. The subscription agreement is similar to a sales contract for more conventional housing.

If you are accepted as a member, you will be required to sign another agreement, often dubbed an occupancy agreement. Also called a proprietary lease, this document spells out how much you will pay in monthly maintenance fees, your responsibilities as a resident and the rules and regulations of the co-op. The occupancy agreement is similar to a lease in a rental unit.

Then you pay the corporation the amount of money you agreed to in return for your stock certificate. This is your portion of ownership in the co-operative. In some co-operatives, the number of shares you receive depends on the size of the unit you occupy. For instance, some co-operatives assess your share in the corporation based on the number of square feet in your living unit.

As a shareholder in the co-operative, you help determine its policies. You have a vote in the election of board members, who usually are in charge of making the day-to-day business decisions of the co-operative. As a resident, you have the right of occupancy of your unit and the use of all mutual facilities.

Co-operatives have established rules and bylaws that are spelled out in the occupancy agreement. Members agree to live by these rules, so be sure you read them thoroughly and agree to the policies before you sign on the dotted line.

Most large co-operatives hire management firms to take care of maintenance and other matters relating to common grounds. If your co-operative has this policy, you will be assessed a monthly carrying charge to cover such operating expenses as maintenance and the salaries of the management staff. This carrying charge is the equivalent of rent and goes toward the monthly mortgage payment on the co-op and property taxes. Another plus of co-operatives is that your carrying charges often will be approximately twenty percent lower than the rent you would pay for a similar apartment.

In addition, you can take some tax deductions on your monthly payments. Those portions of your carrying charges that are used to pay interest on the mortgage payment and to pay taxes are deductible.

Most co-operative stock does not appreciate as much as a single-family home would. Your stock value increases by the amount you pay on the principal each year and the co-operative improvements made on the property and the community. Visit with management and co-operative members before you buy, to find out about the appreciation potential of your particular corporation.

Although co-ops with any number of units can succeed and have succeeded, most experts recommend complexes with 225 to 300 units. When larger, they tend to lose the community spirit. At the 225- and 300-unit range the co-operative generally is small enough to allow all the members to become acquainted, and they're large enough to survive financially. In this size range, some co-operatives offer auxiliary services. Food buying and child care co-operatives are available to residents of conventional housing in some com-

munities.

Today the U.S. boasts about 500,000 co-op units, ranging from subsidized units at $500 per share to posh units ringing up a cool million on the cash register. Government officials predict that thousands of co-operative associations will be formed nationwide within the next ten years.

The average share in stock in the 500 HUD-insured co-operatives now costs about $2,500. An HUD-insured co-operative is one in which the mortgage loan is guaranteed by HUD. Lenders usually are far more willing to make loans for the HUD-backed mortgages than for more conventional ones.

In New York City, where co-operatives are really catching on, a small, conventionally financed co-operative unit may cost between $35,000 and $70,000, with a monthly carrying charge running from $250 to $600. At the Watergate in Washington, made famous by the well known break-in, shares can cost anywhere from $500,000 to $1 million.

To combat the increasing costs of renting, a number of New York apartment tenants are buying buildings from their landlords and converting them into co-operatives. The city offers assistance in converting older rental buildings in the so-called "sweat equity" or "moderate rehab" units. In these co-ops, the residents do a large portion of the physical labor involved in the rehabilitation and renovation work.

New York co-operative conversions face zoning restrictions and financing obstacles. City officials tend to resist rezoning light industrial or commercial areas, so be prepared to convince them that in many cases co-operative pioneers actually are developing the city's resources and recreating neighborhoods where schools and small business can flourish once again.

Bankers are also cautious of such conversions. They don't want to invest several hundred thousand dollars in an unconventional project that may prove to be a boondoggle. As an alternative, loans often come from the former land-lords. Sometimes the tenants take over the existing mortgage from the landlord. Whatever the financing route, you probably need the advice of financial and legal experts to protect your interests.

For years, the growth of co-operatives in this country was limited because they were black-balled by mortgage lenders and builders as nonprofit enterprises. Although it's still not easy to find a nonprofit corporation as a sponsor, co-operatives are flourishing in the cities out of economic necessity.

A number of landlords are finding that it's no longer profitable for them to own large apartment complexes. In some cases, tenant unrest and laws changing the depreciation schedule of apartment complexes, can make ownership a money-losing deal.

Landlords have few options open to them. They can sell a building outright to another landlord. They can convert the project into a condominium. Or they can offer the complex to a co-operative. A number of them are considering the last route the most practical.

In addition to taking over existing mortgages or getting a second mortgage, co-operative buyers also may borrow money to pay for their shares with an HUD-insured loan. As more co-operative conversions occur, co-operatives may provide sound housing alternatives, as well as the benefits of property ownership, to many more Americans.

Another advantage of co-operatives is the tax break. As an average, a $500 monthly maintenance charge on a co-operative is half tax deductible. (The exact amount varies between thirty and seventy percent, depending on the building.) If monthly interest on the bank loan totals $300, then before taking taxes into account you are paying about $800 a month for the apartment. But after you account for taxes, you could be paying the equivalent of $494, according to prominent economist Andrew Tobias.

Constructing new co-operatives is still proba-

Condominiums are becoming the homes of a large number of urban dwellers. In 1977, condominium production totaled 200,000 units, 100,000 of which were in new multi-unit buildings.
Photo: Rita Tatum.

bly ten or twenty years in the future. Presently, the Foundation for Cooperative Housing is the largest American sponsor of co-operatives.

Technically, co-operatives and condominiums are two different housing animals. With a co-operative, you buy shares of stock in a corporation owned jointly with the other tenants. You lease your apartment from that corporation, but you don't own it. Therefore, you cannot mortgage it, although you may borrow against the value of your stock. And you cannot depreciate whatever part of the co-operative you might use for business.

With a condominium, you own the apartment itself, and you have the right to finance it and rent it out to whomever you please, much as if it were a private home. Corporations may not purchase co-operatives, but they can purchase condominiums.

City Lofts

The form of "sweat equity" that has received so much press attention recently is the movement in New York to convert old factories and warehouses into co-operatives. Originating in the Soho section in the early 1960s, this movement became popular when artists began converting old buildings in a predominantly industrial area into working and living quarters.

Many artists began by renting their lofts from the owner. This proved unsatisfactory for the tenant. Once the artist had cleaned and scoured the upper floors, often covered with thirty years of leather scraps, paper shreds or paint chips, the landlords raised the rent so high that the artist had to move out often leaving the landlord with new electrical wiring and modern heating and air conditioning.

To combat this, artists and other loft dwellers consolidated their efforts. They decided to buy the buildings outright, and then convert them into co-operatives. As more and more of these conversions proved successful, other New Yorkers began following the loft dwellers' pioneering efforts. Soon all parts of the city found like-minded people teaming up to form corporations, buy buildings and create co-operatives.

Not everything comes up roses in lofts and co-operatives. Although you may have enough dirt to plant a pastoral glade in your own living room, you probably will want to start with bare floors. Just finding the floor under pounds of debris left by the former manufacturing tenant can involve a great deal of work. You could spend months cleaning out the clutter and installing modern electrical wiring, toilets and other amenities to make your home livable. You start with a raw loft which should cost from $15,000 to $40,000 or more.

Renovating the loft and bringing it up to city housing code standards might cost anywhere from $10,000 to $100,000, depending on the extent of renovation necessary and the amount of space you're rehabbing. In addition, you have to put in money for common work on the building. The building may need the installation of a heating plant, water heater, water lines, or electricity. It could need a facade face-lift or a reroofing job.

You have to understand that in loft conversions, you're probably biting off an enormous do-it-yourself job. Lofts aren't legal living quarters unless they meet apartment building codes in your city. You may be facing costly modifications just to meet the building code. To offset these expenses, look for a warehouse or factory that is going for much less than the amount you'd pay to buy a standard apartment building.

Lenders often don't like to make loans for loft conversions. All they stand to gain if you forfeit is a share of stock for security. You may have to borrow money from less business-like sources, such as your friends, relatives or godparents if you decide that loft living is your alternative.

With a condominium, you own the apartment itself, and you have the right to finance it and rent it out to whomever you please, much as if it were a private home. Nor is there a stigma attached to owning a condominium. This Chicago condominium high rise houses some of the finest families in Chicago.
Photo: Rita Tatum.

Chapter 9

Round Can Be Beautiful and Practical, Too

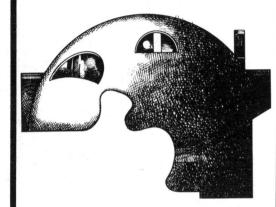

Facing page:
Domes require standard foundation techniques. Per square or lineal foot, the cost should be no more than slab or foundation costs for more ordinary housing. But because of the dome's unusual shape, dome dwellers frequently like to accent it in open sites like this one by Solar Domes Inc.

The one-time darling of rebellious home builders, the dome home now is gaining prestige with the average American family. In the mid-1950s, the geodesic dome became popular on the housing circuit. That is, the concept became popular. Few actual homes were built then. It wasn't until the "tumultuous sixties" that the dome found a place of its own. For a generation geared to protesting the Viet Nam War and other apparent inequities in the American way of life, the dome home represented a different lifestyle. Now all of that is changing.

"At the mid-point of the 1970s, a change in the type of customer interested in dome home living took place," said William Hensel, chairman of the National Association of Dome Home Manufacturers. "In 1977, professional dome home companies noticed that there were far fewer lifestyle types buying domes. Instead, there were many more 'normal' people buying them. Normal people being those with families, average incomes and financing through conventional means."

Hensel said that currently about twenty percent of dome home building goes to the recreational market, for vacation retreats. The remainder of sales, generally in the $50,000 and up class, is being used for year-round living.

While Easterners are not currently jumping on the dome home bandwagon, the geodesic structures made popular by Buckminster Fuller on college campuses only a decade earlier are cropping up all over the Midwest, Southwest and West today.

Dome homes are manufactured by approximately sixty firms throughout the country. (For dome home manufacturers' addresses, see page 151.) Their output ranges from small, no-frills structures to elaborate homes that merge two or more basic dome units. Although they still hold only a tiny share of the massive housing market, dome home manufacturers contend their structures will become increasingly popular. About three times more dome homes were bought and built in 1978 than in 1977.

Construction Economy

One of the reasons for the burgeoning popularity of dome homes is that they are relatively economical to build. Because their total exterior space is the least possible to contain a given volume of space, domes also are easy to heat and cool. Since they contain no bearing walls or columns on the interior, dome homes are flexible enough to suit many people's tastes. The total home can be left open or partitioned off as the family chooses, opening new vistas in living experiences.

Because the self-supporting structure requires no interior walls, many dome dwellers prefer the spacious feeling of an open-plan design. Unconstrained by corners and walls, domes are offered with an almost infinite variety of floor plans and living levels. Some even incorporate a balcony or a full second floor. With a dome there is less base for the enclosed volume than with any other shape of house, which means that owners pay for less wasted space.

Provided your local building code is met, decks, poured walls, concrete block, full basements, concrete slabs, pressure-treated wood foundations or crawl spaces may be used in dome building. In fact, any type of foundation used in conventional housing may be used for a dome home. When done by a qualified contractor, the cost should be very close to that of a foundation for a conventional project with the same outside dimensions or perimeter. Plumbing also is conventional and should pose no unusual problems.

Domes also feature excellent window lighting. Because of more efficient heating and cooling, the structure is quite adaptable to future applications of wind generators, methane generators and wood heating equipment. Some solar collectors are designed for use alongside dome homes. Wood-burning heating systems with hydronic baseboard units heated by the fireplace are already used by some owners.

Compared to similar housing floor space, most domes will need smaller capacity heating and cooling equipment. In fact, warm air, hot water

and steam, solar power, electricity, gas and oil are currently in use in some domes. The average forty-foot diameter dome has a heat loss factor of only 15,000 to 20,000 BTUs.

Power ventilation systems often are recommended to prevent frosting of windows and possible structural damage. In addition, good ventilation increases the effectiveness of air conditioning and heating. Most are installed quickly and are quiet and completely automatic.

As in conventional housing, wiring is housed in walls and floors. In many dome designs, the riser wall provides a convenient wirechase. Track lighting and other modern lighting systems also can be incorporated into domes.

Energy Savings
Just by the nature of its design, a dome is an energy-saving structure. Conventional housing is rectangular or square in shape, while the dome is rounded. If you remember your high school geometry, you know that a circle with the same area as a square has a much smaller perimeter. That perimeter, or exterior, is where a great deal of energy is lost in heating and cooling.

There are some items you may wish to consider adding to cut energy requirements even further. With the skyrocketing cost of future energy, this is not a matter to be dismissed lightly. As a plus, the correct insulation in a dome can save you more than the same insulation in a non-dome with the same floor space.

One type of insulation to consider is fiberglass batting. The batting may be stapled and cut. It can be installed with a vapor barrier similar to its installation in any other well designed building.

Polyfoam sheeting may be glued and cut. In some cases, it can also be installed with a vapor barrier. However, this material must be cut from undersized sheets and is both time-consuming and costly. In addition, if left unprotected, some of this material represents an extreme fire hazard.

Urethane foam, an excellent insulator and weather protector, may be used without a vapor barrier and can be left exposed to the elements. But, possibly more important, it can be a fire hazard in unprotected applications. Most dome builders do not recommend this form of blown-in insulation, because the material has a tendency to settle after time. The resulting pockets, if not properly monitored, could cause large heat losses.

Probably one of the best insulators for dome homes is urea-formaldehyde foam. The material is less flammable than urethane foam and doesn't cause expansion damage. If the quality and type of seam-sealing done on the panels is good, you'll have a fantastic insulation package.

Since water from the outside can damage most insulation, you will need a vapor barrier. When required, a four- to six-mil poly vapor should be applied under the interior panels. If you plan to use wood-heating equipment, which many dome dwellers opt for, foil-faced kraft paper is a good vapor barrier.

The Variables
Provided the original dome construction is sound and compatible, dome dwellers have the option of expanding their home as time and money permit. One popular concept requires building a rather large unit at the outset and adding a second floor or loft later, when your pocketbook can afford it. Another idea that appeals to a number of dome dwellers features separate structures for various activities, such as a living unit dome, a kitchen/mechanical unit and sleeping units. In many cases, gaining more space is as simple as adding another dome.

Dome exteriors are almost as varied as those used in conventional housing. Among the more popular exterior covering systems now in use are cedar shakes, lead-tab shingles and fiberglass. Asphalt shingles probably form the cheapest dome-covering system; they maintain a good seal as well. Cedar shakes and wood shingles are the most attractive. Their heavy texture gives the

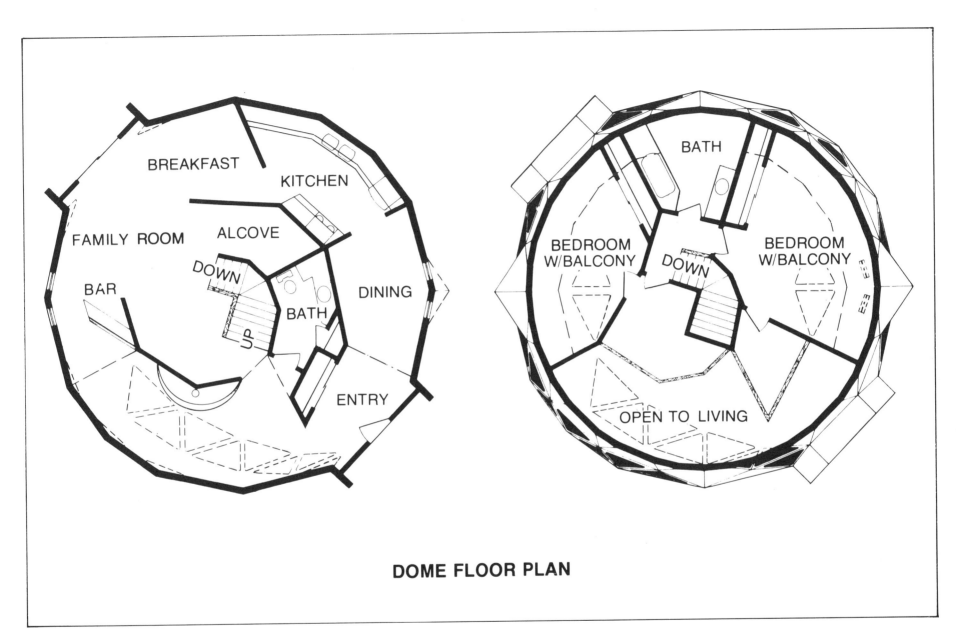

DOME FLOOR PLAN

Built by Domes/Geodyssey
Corporation, this 40½ foot
dome home offers a very flexible interior because the inside does not require supporting walls.
Drawing by Ken Nash

Round Can Be Beautiful and Practical, Too

dome a rustic look, blending nicely with heavily wooded sites. They are more expensive, though, because shakes require a great deal of on-site labor to apply.

Dome shells come in a variety of sizes to suit nearly anyone's space requirements. Smaller domes, often 26½ feet in diameter, offer a full first level plus a loft—about 525 square feet of living space altogether. Because the total square footage in these domes is limited, many people choose them for vacation retreats.

If you're looking for a first home, you'll probably want to consider either the 40½-foot diameter dome or the larger, 45½-foot style. The 40-foot diameter dome offers 1,200 feet of space on the first floor and about 950 square feet on the second. The 45½-foot dome provides nearly 1,600 square feet of space on the first floor and about 1,400 square feet on the second floor. These are the most popular sizes for home living, but there's enough variety that a little shopping around should lead you to exactly the amount of floor space you need.

Domes require standard foundation techniques. Per square or lineal foot, the cost should be no more than slab or foundation costs for any other normal structure. Most companies use standard western floor framing for the first floor of the dome and post and beam framing for the loft or second floor. Floor plates or riser walls are installed on the floor foundation with standard construction procedures. If you choose a box-beam riser, you will also have an ideal plumbing and wiring chase.

Building Steps

Although you might run across what looks like advanced calculus in some dome home literature, most companies use either 2 x 4 or 2 x 6 panel frames that assemble quickly with little or no heavy equipment other than the contractor's scaffolding and step ladders. In fact, a number of dome manufacturers feel that the higher mathematics of dome building should be left in the plant. They are concerned that complex equations could confuse rather than enlighten consumers.

After the framing is completed, one-piece exterior panels are nailed and glued to the frame's exterior. Skylights, standard dormers—windows and framing that project through the sloped framing of the roof—and doors are also installed at this point. The seams are then sealed, and the dormers are sealed with a special adhesive.

Plumbing and electrical wiring are installed inside, through the superstructure and floors. Then a four- to six-mil poly or kraft paper vapor barrier is generally installed on the inside of the frame. Firring strips are applied to the inside of the structure.

If you have selected urea formaldehyde foam as the insulator, two-inch diameter holes are drilled from the exterior into each panel. Then the foam is installed and the holes are plugged. At this point, all interior work, as well as the installation of the loft or second floor, may begin.

For conventional roofing, two layers of felt paper are applied to the dome's exterior. Then tab shingles or cedar shakes are installed to the client's specifications.

For those of you interested in maximum energy conservation, up to 6½ inches of insulation can be installed between the exterior and interior panels. With some insulations, the resulting "R" factor would exceed R-35 for the entire dome shell. (The R factor is an expression of insulating efficiency. The higher the R factor, the better the insulation being rated.) In fact, one forty-foot diameter, all-electric dome home was rated by an upper Midwest electric company as the most economical electrically-heated home in the climate zone.

Taking the Options

Many companies offer a wide range of optional equipment for dome homes. Some of the more common items include monolithic interior panels, insulated sealed-in panel windows, decorator

FRONT (NW) ELEVATION   SCALE 1'-4'-0' 148

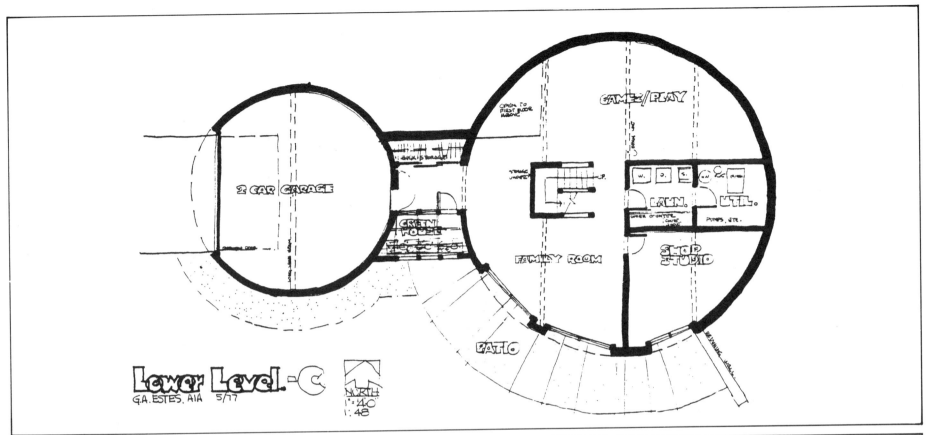

Lower Level - C
G.A. ESTES, AIA   5/77

NORTH
1" = 4'-0"
1:48

2 CAR GARAGE

GREEN HOUSE

OPEN TO FIRST FLOOR ABOVE

GAMES/PLAY

FAMILY ROOM

LAUN.

UTL.

PUMPS, ETC.

SHOP STUDIO

PATIO

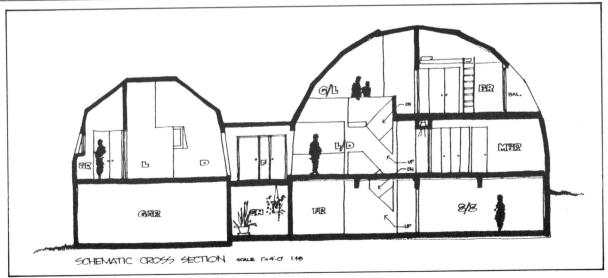

SCHEMATIC CROSS SECTION   SCALE 1"=4'-0" 1:48

GAR

GH

FR

B/B

This page and overleaf:

Front and rear elevations, section, floor plans, and window detailing for the Feldsien residence built by Solar Domes, Inc.
Courtesy of Solar Domes, Inc.

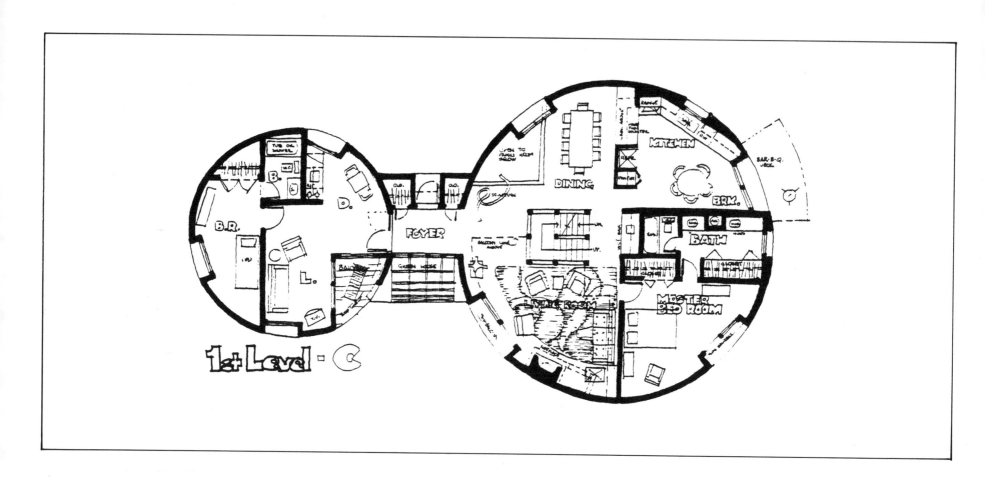

1st Level - C

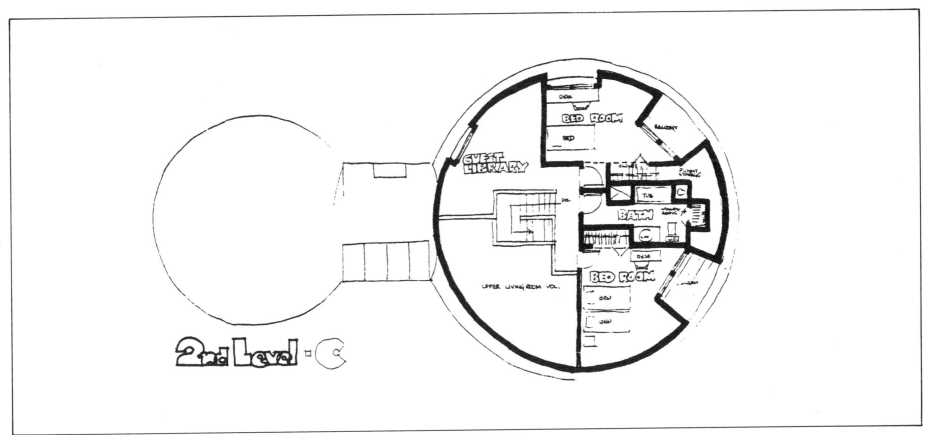

BED ROOM

BALCONY

GUEST LIBRARY

BATH

TUB

UPPER LIVING ROOM VOL.

BED ROOM

2nd Level ⬤C

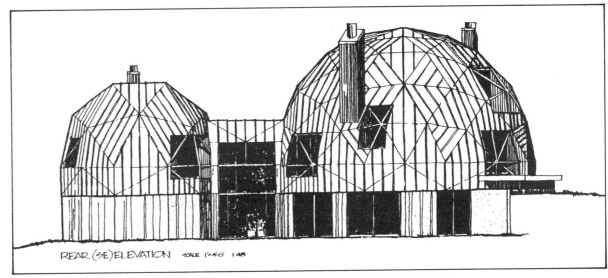

REAR (SE) ELEVATION   SCALE 1"=4'-0" 1:48

Round Can Be Beautiful and Practical, Too

The beauty of a dome home, like this one built by Dome Home Systems Inc., is accented at night when the unusual window shapes dominate the rounded architectural shape.

finished cowlings, exterior dormer systems, all-weather wood foundations and garages. As in the design of any new home, what and how much you add to your dome is a personal matter, limited only by the reaches of your imagination. Embellishments can range from built-in, automated appliances to energy-saving devices and intricate decorating touches. One company even markets a composting waste handling system that aerobically breaks down waste into bacteria-free fertilizer.

Monolithic interior panels, for example, add strength and beauty to domes. These versatile panels may be fireproofed, painted, stained, antiqued, spray-textured, wiped or two-toned—each giving a distinctively different effect.

Insulated, sealed-in panel windows often can be installed and tempered at the plant in any standard panel of the dome shell. They can offer a creative opportunity and give a mark of originality to your home. They also are an energy plus, if carefully designed for solar heating and skylighting. Correctly placed, these windows provide an unmatched view of the outside, as well as offering heat and light during the desired seasons.

Traditional, rectangular windows often can be chosen for dome homes. But you also might want to consider using triangles, circles and trapezoid-shaped versions. Some companies also provide optional solar gray or bronze glass, which can cut heat loss through windows by as much as fifty percent. For the best energy savings, make sure the solar windows have an integral tinting, not a surface coating. Your architect can recommend the type of window system that is best for your particular climate. For most buildings, all glass units should be at least ⅝-inch thick, insulated and flat-tempered.

Some companies even offer decorator-finished cowlings to match your countertops, furniture and interior decor. Dormer systems for standard three-foot-wide doors, patio doors and upstairs and downstairs opening windows also are available. If you are interested, make sure panels and

framing are precut and coded at the plant to avoid confusion during the field installations.

Your local contractor can offer you the option of all-weather wood foundations. Ask him or her where else the foundation has been installed successfully. Incorrectly installed wood foundations can leak and warp, causing the home owner untold migraines and expensive retrofitting. You'll also need to make sure wood foundations are permitted by your local building code.

If you're interested in a garage to match your home, many companies offer a smaller dome shell. A good size is twenty-six feet in diameter. You also may want to make sure the garage dome is provided with dormer system for a twelve-foot by seven-foot overhead door.

Contractors and Building Codes

Be particularly careful to choose a contractor who understands the dome building concept thoroughly. There have been, and still are, some domes around that feature indoor rain every time there are thundershowers. However, proper sealing eliminates this leakage. A well-constructed dome is as waterproof as more traditional housing.

Shell costs are far less for domes than they are for other types of housing, because less material is used. The panels are frequently preformed and cut at the factory, saving on-site labor hours. However, more time is necessary to finish dome interiors. Nevertheless, the average saving on finished cost for a dome home structure is between eight and ten percent.

Most dome designs fall within standard building codes. Some styles, however, could need slight modifications to meet your local building department's standards, so be sure to check before you go ahead.

If you live in the Midwest, you may be concerned about snow loading. Many dome shells are designed to withstand a forty-pound per square foot snow load and a twenty-pound per square inch windload/deadload. Conventional housing in

Because they have less surface area to lose heat, the correct insulation in a dome home can save you more money in energy power costs than the same insulation in a non-dome building. This snug little home in the Midwest was built by Dannenburg Construction.

Round Can Be Beautiful and Practical, Too

To give you some idea of a dome home interior, the following five pictures are the Feldsien residence, built by Solar Domes, Inc.

Interior view of the living room.

Facing page:
Interior view of the dining area.
Photo by Kalivoda, courtesy of Solar Domes, Inc.

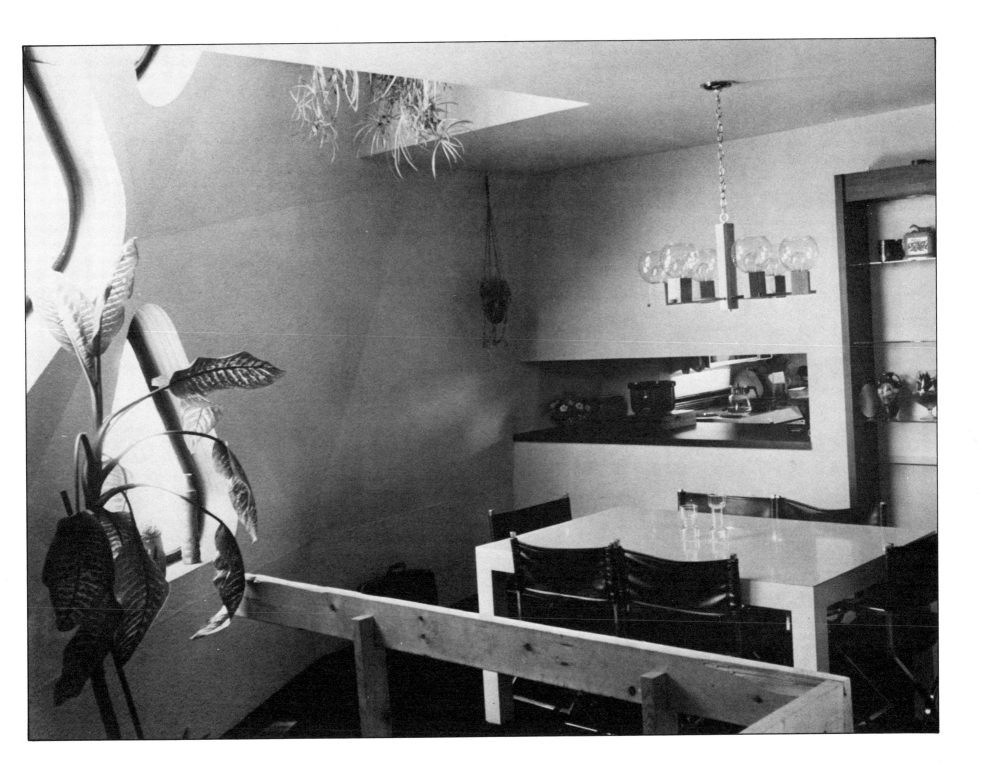

Round Can Be Beautiful and Practical, Too

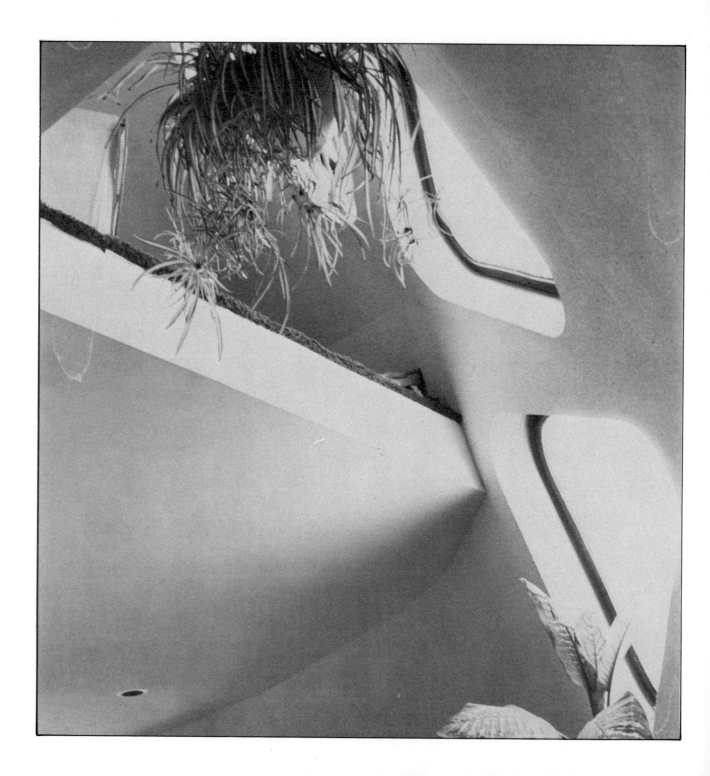

View up to the loft.
Photo by Kalivoda, courtesy of Solar Domes, Inc.

Above facing page:
View up from the living room to the top of the dome, showing stairwell and balcony railings.
Photo by Kalivoda, courtesy of Solar Domes, Inc.

Bottom facing page:
Loft area.
Photo by Kalivoda, courtesy of Solar Domes, Inc.

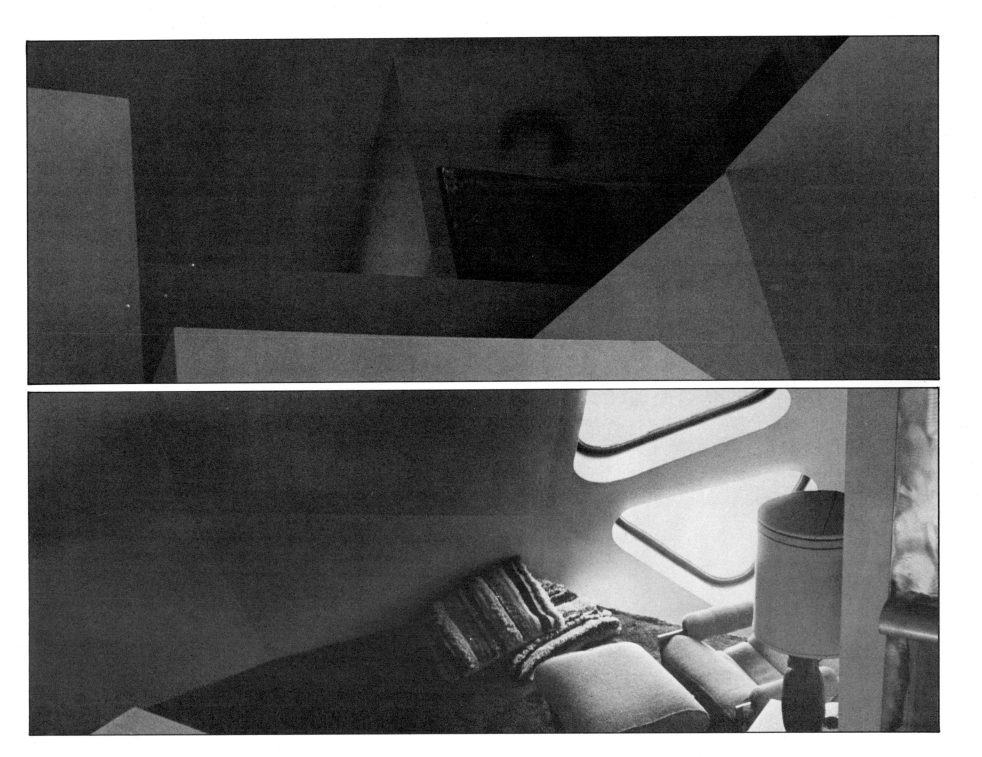

Round Can Be Beautiful and Practical, Too

Contrary to some of the literature available, the skill level in erecting a dome is at least as important in erecting a dome as it is in any other home construction. If you are not well versed in construction, the best thing you can do is hire a professional architect and/or contractor. Photo courtesy of the National Association of Dome Home Manufacturers.

Facing page:
Dome interiors frequently capture the personalities of their owners. While the exterior of this home by Domes America, Inc., is very futuristic, the interior is done in a more traditional manner.

the Midwest is generally designed for a forty-pound snow load, with a built-in safety factor.

Contrary to some of the dome literature you may have read, the skill level in erecting a dome is as important as it is in any other home construction. The average house building crew will reach a peak on the learning curve after they have completed the third house shell of the same size. Skill improvement on finishing work proceeds more slowly and often depends on the detail of the working drawings. For this reason, it's a good idea to look at some of the other domes the contractor has erected. Some manufacturers will recommend local contractors they know understand dome building.

You may also want to investigate your local lending institutions carefully. Some lenders may require you to pay up to fifty percent of the cost before they'll underwrite a loan on something they consider a nontraditional and therefore risky venture. Others may contend that they cannot predict the market value or resale potential of a dome home. So they, too, will decline the loan.

Since many lending institutions are becoming interested in loaning money for energy-saving units, you may be able to sell them on the dome's energy conservation features. Still others will offer you conventional, eighty-percent mortgage loans for domes, based on detailed drawings and your credit rating. But you may have to shop around for financing to get the best mortgage.

Because domes are still offbeat, newspapers often cover local success stories featuring dome home building by the owner. Often they imply that the owner needed little or no expertise in home building, and that the only tools necessary were hammer and nails. Cost figures also may include just the shell figure, not what was actually spent to complete the home.

Dome Home Kits

If you're up to a challenge, you might consider using a dome home kit. But be careful—it's far

from easy. With twenty years of experience under his hardhat, one Chicago home building contractor said he would not tackle a dome shell until he had done his homework. While you can conceivably save $6,000 to $8,000 by constructing your own home, you also could be throwing your money down the drain. One Wisconsin owner spent between $45,000 and $50,000 on a "kit" that still doesn't work properly. In fact, he cannot even live in the home. Others, however, have successfully completed kits with only marginal problems.

Before you rush out to buy a kit and assemble your own home, you should check out all the angles thoroughly. "It's rather like selling someone the body of a car. You wing it from there to get it running," pointed out William Hensel, chairman of the National Association of Dome Home Manufacturers. "Sure, there are simple directions to put it together. But where do you go for the expertise necessary to construct the engine?"

If you still plan to tackle a kit, know what you're getting for your hard-earned money. For instance, how many panels are supplied in the kit? Are they 2 x 4s or 2 x 6s? Does the insulation come with it or is it optional? How much will you pay for the freight? Are there interior panels? Are they one-piece units or spliced? What kind of foundation is necessary? Will your home meet your local building code?

If you're not well versed in construction, the best thing you can do is hire a professional architect or contractor. He or she can carefully go over all the material and check for any possible snags. (See Chapter 3 for more information on finding an architect.)

Avoiding the Pitfalls

In your research, obtain literature from as many dome home component suppliers as possible. Before you sign anything, here are some guidelines to follow in purchasing a dome home.

Remember that the purchase of the dome home shell is just one small step in erecting a

site-built house. It's like buying the body of a Datsun 280Z, sans engine and wheels. A relative youngster to the housing industry, dome home building is still complex. Someday you may be able to buy a dome and have it assembled on the site in two days. But today you cannot, simply because the fine points in housing take years to sand down. Generally, the purchase of the dome's manufactured components accounts for less than twenty-five percent of the home's finished cost. So if you think you are saving $20,000 or more, think again. Something is obviously missing, probably the "guts" of your home.

Reputable companies will spell out usable floor space for you. That is the only way to evaluate a dome. The diameter is not an indication of floor space or of value.

To lay out the interior of your home, some companies offer planning aids such as scaled floor plans with furniture templates and model kits. Most have a portfolio of existing and proposed floor plans that may help you figure out your own room arrangements.

If you discover any mathematics you don't understand, ask the company to explain its dimensions in standard language. Dome homes are relatively new, and they do feature more complicated construction details than stick-built housing. Reputable companies don't expect their customers to be Einsteins.

Before you purchase anything, take the drawings and plans to a local contractor. Try to have him pinpoint a finished cost for you. Then approach your financial institution for further recommendations.

Possibly buoyed by local press coverage of a successful dome in your area, some financial institutions may be quite willing to lend money for such ventures. Others, who may have been burned by a $12,000 dome that ended up costing $50,000, may laugh you right out the front door. Don't be daunted. If one bank turns you down, another may be more receptive.

Domes have been paid for and financed with all the methods used in conventional home build-

ing. Some owner-builders sell existing homes, using the equity to pay for most of the dome materials. Conventional first mortgages also have been obtained, usually from the dome dweller's local bank or savings and loan. These facilities also can provide mortgages insured by FHA or through GI or VA programs. (These applications, however, often require extensive drawings and the applicant must meet credit qualifications.) Credit unions, insurance companies and finance companies also are sources of money for shorter, five- to fifteen-year loans.

Be sure to hire a qualified architect, local to your homesite. If you trust your contractor, you can ask him or her to recommend an architect. If not, select one from your area. A good place to start looking for a qualified architect is the nearest chapter of the American Institute of Architects. (A listing of local chapters can be found on page 148.) Even if the company you're purchasing the dome components from has qualified architects on its staff, they are probably 2,000 miles away at the manufacturing plant, drafting standard designs and handling slight modifications. They will not know that your homesite is former marshland, or that your local building code requires footings for any structure more than one story tall. The local architect will be familiar with these conditions, and he or she will know what is necessary to pass local building codes and receive building permits.

If you are interested in assisting in the construction, find out what help is supplied with the dome shell. Even if you plan to hire a local contractor, you may wish to find out how he will be trained to erect your home. Unless he's specialized in dome home building, which is not likely, he too will have some questions on construction details and the proper erection order of components, proper sealants, additional insulation, etc.

Finally, find out just how much the total home is going to cost. Include in that figure all of the items you would expect if you were going the more traditional housing route.

Even under construction,
dome homes like this one from
Solar Domes, Inc., have a
clearly futuristic look.
Photo by Kalivoda, courtesy
of Solar Domes, Inc.

Chapter 10

Log Cabins Are Not Just for Pioneers

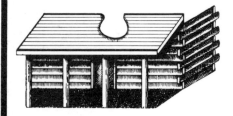

The history of our country reflects the significant contribution made by homes built of logs. In the pioneering days of Daniel Boone and Davy Crockett, the log cabin offered protection and comfort. Today the closest most Americans come to experiencing the total, enduring atmosphere of a log house is the fleeting aura forged by the flames of wood-burning fireplaces. That is, until they discover that the little old cabin of yesteryear has grown into a charming, rustic, easy-to-maintain, modern home.

Once a symbol of humble beginnings, the log cabin has risen more than a notch or two in status. Today's log homes are modern and spacious. In fact, they're nothing like the home that sheltered Abraham Lincoln as he did his math before the fire. Today's log home dwellers calculate their checkbook balances with electronic calculators. They often find that their rustic residences appreciate in value at least as rapidly as more conventional housing.

Many manufacturers and dealers stress economy as a key reason for choosing a log home over a more conventionally framed house. Manufacturers point out quickly that a log home is easy to build. Often sold as kits, the log package comes with coded logs, doors and windows as well as step-by-step instructions. (For a listing of manufacturers of log homes, see page 152.)

A log home really can be inexpensive to build. Prices for the kits range from approximately $10,000 for a basic, three-bedroom home to more than $35,000 for a custom, six-bedroom design incorporating the ultimate in log cabin luxury. You should be aware, however, that the finished house may cost two to three times the price of the exterior or shell package. Nevertheless, log construction is said to be slightly cheaper and much sturdier than a conventional house. Conservation estimates suggest you can save five percent by building a log home as opposed to buying a conventionally framed house.

Provided it's properly sealed, a log home also can be cheaper to heat. Those dealers who claim logs are fuel savers point out that the prepackaged variety is well insulated during the actual building process. Logs interlock for a tight fit. One company, New England Log Homes of Hamden, Connecticut, claims its 8- to 10½-inch logs have six times the insulation capacity of common brick. The company also points out that one inch of log is equal to 1,400 inches of aluminum in insulating properties. A thick, solid log wall could result in a substantial R value. (R is a measure of a material's ability to resist heat loss.) A definite R value is difficult to determine for log homes, since the logs are somewhat irregular, with varying diameters. In addition, many log homes use fireplaces and Franklin stoves to supply part of the heating requirements. So energy savings can be tied partially to the use of unconventional fuel sources.

Most log cabin dwellers agree that a log home is easier to maintain. No one in his or her right mind would paint or paper a log wall. The surrounding natural wood adds a warmth to the home that can rarely be duplicated with paint or wallpaper.

Some owners have built their homes in heavily wooded areas, far from the bustle of city or suburban life. Others have penetrated the otherwise conventional suburbs with log homes. If you do choose to construct your log home in a standard suburban subdivision, be prepared for gawkers all through the week. Log homes still hold a fascination for the uninitiated.

Some Wooden Facts

If you are seriously considering a log home, you may want to know some facts about the building material that has been used as long as man has constructed homes. Under a microscope, you can see that wood is composed of thousands of hollow cells, formed from tiny cellulose fibers. A single cubic inch of wood contains about three million cellulose fibers. These fibers and the cells they form are bonded tightly with a natural glue called lignin. As a matter of fact, lignin bonds so tena-

Log Cabins Are Not Just for Pioneers

ciously that for years scientists thought cellulose and lignin were one and the same.

Surprisingly, wood also has incredible strength. In fact, wood is stronger—pound for pound—than steel. This strength comes from the strength of the wood cells. The lignin that bonds the cells together is not only strong, but is also elastic. So wood gives, which explains why wooden floors are less tiring to walk on than concrete. It also explains why wood can bend without breaking under the stress of high winds or earthquakes.

According to the American Wood Council, a concrete wall would have to be five feet thick to equal the insulating quality of just four inches of wood. That's because wood isn't as dense as it looks. Its cells contain millions of tiny air spaces. Trapped air is the best insulator known. So, wood homes keep you warmer in the winter and cooler in the summer. A test conducted at Arizona State University showed that wood could actually help reduce heating and cooling bills. The test compared the fuel consumption of two structures that were identical in size. While one was constructed of wood, the other featured masonry construction. Both structures were insulated. In the test, both structures were exposed simultaneously to identical weather conditions and controlled interior temperatures.

During the heating season, the wood house used twenty-three percent less fuel than the masonry house. During the air conditioning period, the wood house consumed thirty percent less fuel in an area where temperatures often soar above one hundred degrees Fahrenheit.

Another endearing characteristic of wood is its lasting ability. The Old Ironworks in Saugus, Massachusetts was completed in 1646. Despite three centuries of New England winters, the house still stands. While not every plank is the original wood, the entire frame is, as are the exterior posts, the sub-flooring and most of the floor. In fact, some of the exterior wooden shingles are more than three centuries old.

Even outdoors, some woods need no maintenance at all. Wood weathers well because its cellular structure is affected only slightly by water and heat. Wood and wood products are also fairly easy to work with. They can be nailed, glued, sawed, screwed and sanded, without great effort or expensive tools. This helps explain why wood houses are so simple and inexpensive to expand and remodel.

Wood's biggest disadvantage is the ravages that can be accomplished by termites. However, if you have your house regularly inspected by qualified termite exterminators, you can keep the damage to a minimum.

The Log Package

Generally, owners of log homes purchase a particular log package, rather than a total home containing all the components for a completed house. With the majority of log home kits, the following parts are offered: precut wall logs; precut second floor joists; precut rafters; precut gable ends; all windows, often including the door jambs; two prehung doors; gaskets; fiberboard splines; ten-inch spikes; windstop; caulking compound; and blueprints.

Homeowners must provide the finishing materials, as well as the roofing and flooring, although some companies offer flooring and roofing as options. The owner also must supply the electrical and plumbing systems, cabinets, foundation, fireplace, subflooring and labor to construct the home.

Generally, precut log homes are shipped Freight on Board (FOB) from the manufacturer's nearest plant. That means that you, the buyer, will need to pay transportation charges. Transportation charges are based on a trailer load, per mile rate. Most log homes require two such trailer loads. You should ask the manufacturer to supply you with estimated freight charges.

Although financing may not be as easy as for more conventional housing, you can usually obtain the same type of mortgage as you would for

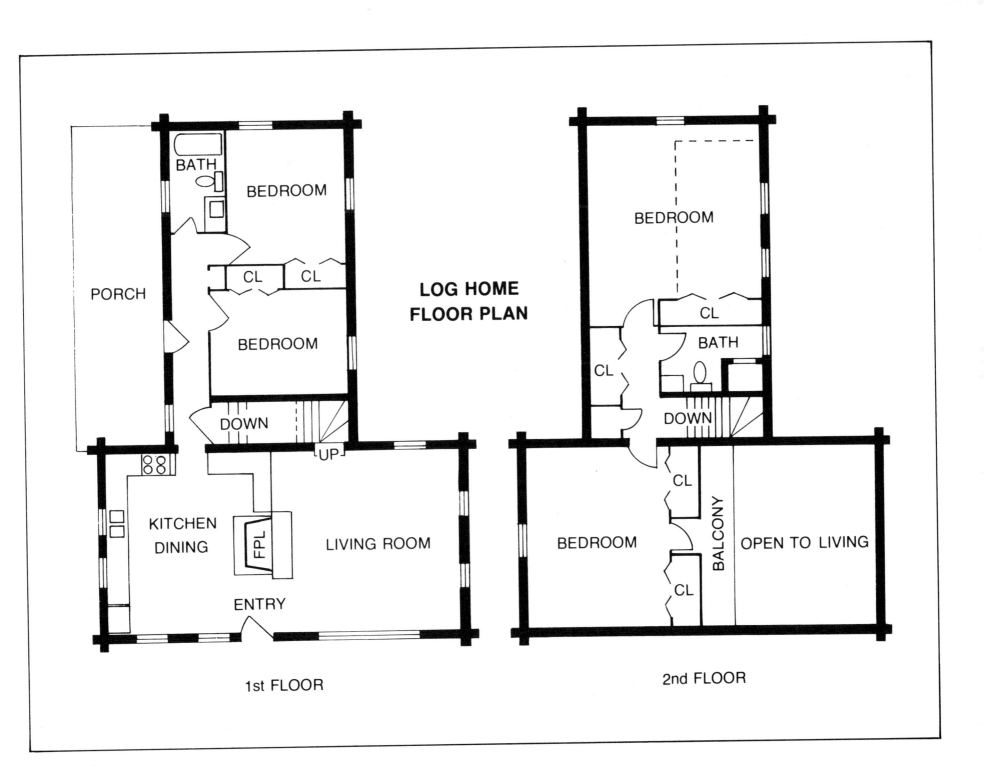

LOG HOME
FLOOR PLAN

1st FLOOR

PORCH

BATH

BEDROOM

CL CL

BEDROOM

DOWN

UP

KITCHEN
DINING

FPL

LIVING ROOM

ENTRY

2nd FLOOR

BEDROOM

CL

BATH

CL

DOWN

CL

BEDROOM

CL

BALCONY

OPEN TO LIVING

another type of home. If you have questions on financing, you may wish to talk with your personal banker as well as the dealer of log homes in your area. Many log homes also have been structurally approved by the Federal Housing Authority (FHA), which qualifies them for FHA-, VA- and HUD-backed financing. Check with the dealer to make sure the home you plan to buy does meet FHA standards.

In the manufacturing plant, precut logs are soaked in a wood preservative, which is both odorless and colorless, and which has proven itself in many applications. Most manufacturers recommend that the homeowner protect the house with repeated applications of the wood preservative on an annual or a biannual basis. To apply the preservative, an ordinary fruit tree sprayer can be used, after you have covered the shrubbery and windows. Interior applications are not needed. The length of time between applications of the wood preservative varies with the location of your home. Homes located in the South will require treatment more frequently than those in the North. Spraying the average house with the preservative will require about a day of your time and twenty gallons of preservative.

Treatment of your log home with a wood preservative will result in a beautiful home that will be able to withstand the weather. Some homeowners also finish exterior logs with linseed oil or polyurethane liquids, but this is not a common practice.

Selecting a Site

If you plan to build a log home, you will have to select the site carefully. The same site that looked beautiful and was easy to reach in the summer might be full of mud and snow in the dead of winter. The lot must be accessible to the sixty-five-foot trailers that will deliver the log home to the site. You also should pay special attention to the positioning of the home, looking for the setting and the view it will allow. Windows should be oriented to allow you the best views and lighting. For instance, morning sunlight filtering into the kitchen can help create a warm and welcome atmosphere during breakfast.

Many log home manufacturers recommend that you install a ten-inch concrete foundation for your home. If you intend to use block construction, eight- to ten-inch blocks, properly constructed and capped, can be used. Your foundation contractor also should install all sill anchor rods, beam pockets, lolly column footings and porch post footings, as described in the blueprints for the log home. If you have a septic system, the tank and field should be set according to your local building code's standards.

Some manufacturers use the two-foot by ten-foot box sill—a standard method of construction—as the primary method of sill construction. This allows increased accessibility to the "A" log for electrical wiring, provides for positive sill anchorage and permits installation of the subfloor and deck before you receive the log package.

After the subflooring is installed over the two-foot by ten-foot joists, the final flooring is laid. Some homeowners prefer placing carpeting over the subflooring. Others prefer the rustic appeal of a solid wood floor. A number of manufacturers suggest hardwood flooring of pine or hemlock. To duplicate the flooring of the pioneer days, some owners prefer wide pine flooring, which is also offered as an option by some manufacturers.

Although you often will be required to provide the roofing, a number of companies offer roofing packages that can be delivered to your building site along with your log package. Frequently, this roofing is constructed of ponderosa pine. If you prefer, you can use handsplit shakes, although their cost is considerably higher.

Generally, windows are delivered to the job site, along with jambs, ready for assembly. The window jambs are assembled at the site and placed in the correct location. Then spreaders are installed between the jambs. When the log pack-

According to the American Wood Council, a concrete wall would have to be five feet thick to equal the insulating quality of just four inches of wood.
Photo: New England Log Homes, Inc.

Log Cabins Are Not Just for Pioneers

age is completely assembled, the spreaders are removed, and the window unit is placed into the opening and nailed to the jambs.

Doors are frequently prehung at the plant, ready for installation. If the natural finish of the doors is to be retained, they should be treated with linseed oil or a high-quality urethane finish. This will keep the door from shrinking and swelling as much as it would if it were not treated.

No log home seems complete without a fireplace. The type and style can be chosen by you. Styles range from brick to flagstone. You should shop around for a fireplace, because the price can vary considerably, depending on the style you choose.

Basically, the heating system installed in a log home is no different than in any other type of house. The homeowner can install hot water baseboard heating systems as well as hot air or electric units. In the South, natural gas and forced air have been proven effective and generally are preferred in this region. The heating elements chosen for your home can be installed after the log package is erected and during completion of the finished carpentry. Some owners install Franklin stoves to supplement their heating requirements. The aroma of smoke and the charm of a cast-iron stove can enhance the decor of any log home.

Before the plumbing is installed, the homeowner must have a "perk" test done to be certain that the soil on which the home is to be built is suitable for a leaching system. A plumber or local building code inspector can give you more information on this leaching system and what it involves for your locale. For log homes not connected to a city's sewage system, a septic system must be installed. The number of residents will dictate the size of septic system you need. To be sure you avoid future problems, make sure the septic system is adequate for all of your present and future needs. Without an effective leaching field, the septic system will not function properly.

A competent electrician will be required for all electrical wiring. The wiring is placed along with "A" course of logs and behind the baseboard. Then electrical outlets are placed in the baseboards, as they are in many conventional houses. If you need a light switch near the door of a room, wire moulding often is used to protect the wiring and to prevent prying little fingers from possible electrocution. Lighting fixtures that hang from the floor joists can also be used in most log homes. In this case, a groove is cut along the top of the floor joist and the wire is placed in the groove. Then a hole is drilled through the floor joist so the wire can run through to the lighting fixture. Wiring and plumbing can be placed within the interior partitions dividing the individual rooms.

Log home manufacturers provide a building manual that is a step-by-step guide to the construction of the home. This manual provides the basic information for the professional builder.

Don't forget to contact your insurance agent for all the necessary insurance coverage you will need. You will need insurance from the time the log package is delivered through the construction and completion of your home.

As with several of the other housing alternatives covered in this book, you may wish to consult an architect before you buy any plans or sign any papers. You'll also want to get legal advice from your attorney and the backing of your personal banker.

Although constructing log homes is not recommended for someone still having trouble tinkering with birdhouse kits, they can be built, provided you have some do-it-yourself experience and a strong back. One couple who used to own a ranch house, said there was no comparison between the two homes: "The ranch had an air about it that wasn't exceptional in cost value and appearance. That's something you don't feel in a log home, when you're surrounded by sturdy, solid pine."

Chapter 11

Factory-Built Housing—It's Come a Long Way

Facing page:
A-frames are one of the popular manufactured housing systems available. Many people consider A-frames as second homes or vacation retreats, because they are economical to construct.
Photo: *Professional Builder.*

After months of fruitless and exhaustive searching for a good house that they can afford, many Americans are discovering factory-built housing. Those tinny, wheeled homes featured ten years ago in Joe's Mobile Home Court on the rough side of town resemble the more modern factory-built homes of today as much as a Model T mirrors a Mercedes-Benz.

Unfortunately, the average family that doesn't own a home today probably never will be able to save enough to buy a conventionally built home—tomorrow, next week or next decade. Besides the cost savings, which vary with the location, many factory-built houses also feature higher construction quality than some traditional housing. The factory-built house also can often be delivered and prepared for occupancy only a few months after the initial order is placed.

These are only a few of the facts behind the factory-built housing boom. In 1977 approximately 600,000 factory-built homes were made and sold in the U.S., according to the National Association of Home Manufacturers. Put another way, one out of every one- and two-family homes being built is factory-constructed.

Bureau of Census figures document the increasing popularity of manufactured housing. In 1971, mobile homes made up seventy-three percent of the market in new homes selling for less than $20,000. By 1976, that market share leaped to ninety-six percent. Similarly, in the less-than-$30,000 class, mobile homes comprised fifty-one percent of the market in 1971 and seventy-six percent by 1976.

Varying in design and construction, factory-built housing offers considerable diversity. The homes can be nearly complete, "mobile" homes, or they can be house packages that require more on-site assembly.

Technically, a *mobile home* is at least eight feet wide and thirty-two feet long. It is built on a permanent chassis with wheels attached. Designed to be transported to the site, a mobile home is constructed literally to stand on its own.

It includes the plumbing, heating, air conditioning and electrical systems necessary, plus all of the connections to attach to the required utilities. A mobile home can be attached to a permanent foundation, and many are. Depending on your preference, the mobile home can be offered fully furnished or not.

The *double-wide mobile home* consists of two sections, combined horizontally at the site. An expandable mobile home has one or more room sections that fold, collapse or telescope into the principal unit during transport. At the site, the expandable portions provide additional living space.

A *modular home* is one that is built in two or more sections in the factory. The plumbing, heating and electrical systems are installed as an integral part of the construction process and are designed to conform to the building codes of the locality where the home is to be situated on a permanent foundation. A modular home includes fewer amenities, such as furniture, than the mobile homes usually offer.

Unlike modular or mobile home systems, the *house package* or *pre-engineered home* generally includes just the exterior of the building. However, a number of companies also provide you with a list of the appliances they have available that you may specify.

An engineered home frequently provides you with a floor system, supporting posts, exterior walls, wall insulation, cavity partitions if necessary, windows, roof and loft beams, roof systems and often a choice of exterior finishes.

One step simpler than the modular home is the *panelized house.* It comes to the site in ready-to-assemble sections such as floors, walls and ceilings.

The *precut house* is produced in the factory by cutting all of the structural components to a specified size, numbering each for its location in the overall plan and shipping the pieces out. The precut house is the major manufactured housing process found in many new subdivisions across

Manufactured homes meet modern housing demands both inside and outside at lower costs. Photo: courtesy of the American Plywood Association.

the country. Because production is kept in the plant, this form of housing eliminates costly and time-consuming cutting of the lumber on the site. It also means that construction is not held up by bad weather during the initial phases, because cutting and measuring is being done in enclosed factories.

At first glance, the precut house may look like just a bunch of lumber in weird sizes and shapes. But if you look more closely, you'll see that all components are part numbered for quick, easy identification, which helps prevent errors and time-consuming uncertainty. In fact, several companies use the same numbering system on the buyer's set of plans, materials list and construction manual. You may be able to visualize exactly how the home fits together. (For more information on exciting precut and panelized housing, see Chapters 9 and 10, on dome and log homes.)

Nearly every piece in the pre-engineered house is cut at the factory, generally to size. All of this preplanning allows a number of pre-engineered buildings to be completed two weeks or so after the parts shipment arrives at the site.

For most systems, the major components of the house interlock. Wall planks, floor and roof decking often are tongue-and-grooved for easier assembly. Although you may wish to check, home building systems are approved by most of the major building codes adopted by many communities.

A number of companies also offer prospective buyers the option of making some modifications to the initial design. If you really plan to significantly modify a pre-engineered house, however, you probably should hire a professional architect to make sure you aren't making changes that won't meet your local building code or soil conditions.

Factory-built houses are manufactured by more than 800 builders throughout the country. Another 2,200 factories manufacture mass-produced sections and components for houses.

(For a listing of mobile/modular home manufacturers, see page 153.) These homes range from a mere $6,000 for a completely furnished, one-bedroom mobile home to more than $125,000 for a sprawling luxury house in a fashionable suburb.

Generally, choosing a modular or factory-built home allows the buyer to save between ten and fifteen percent as compared to the price of a conventional home of similar size. In many cases, factory-built housing can be ordered from a local dealer's catalog and be delivered and ready for move-in just three to four weeks later.

Modular housing does have some drawbacks, however. One, unfortunately, is that some cities, such as Chicago and New York, have outdated building codes that will not allow factory-built housing within the city limits. Of course, lot prices in major metropolitan areas often would preclude consideration of modular housing anyway. If you have the money to afford that $20,000 lot, you probably also have the money to hire an architect and have the house completely custom designed.

In some parts of the country, factory-built housing is almost as expensive as site-built units, although this is slowly changing, too. The reason for the cost is often tied to the manufacturer's costs in selling the concept of factory-manufactured housing. In addition, sometimes the local dealer/builder may deliberately set up his price to more closely parallel conventional housing prices in his locale.

Manufactured housing is about as different as people are. Styles range from such traditional designs as Cape Cods and colonial models to modern ranch and contemporary homes. There also are one-story, two-story and split-level versions, geared to meet nearly anyone's taste.

Frequently, factory-built houses are bought through local dealer/builders who arrange for delivery and completion of the house. In addition, a growing number of land developers are putting up whole subdivisions. These subdivisions closely resemble regular developments, except they are

Located in Waverly, New York, this manufactured home accents unfinished wood and makes a strong, boxy visual architectural statement as well. Notice the window treatment and the sharply angular accents created by the panels.

Manufactured housing is built in the factory.
Photo: courtesy of the American Plywood Association.

stocked with the factory-made models. Often priced under other subdivisional housing, manufactured houses in land developments are bought complete on their lots. Some experts in home building trends predict this form of construction represents the way of the future in land developments.

With the exception of modular, prefabricated houses, mobile homes are probably the only forms of single-family housing that can be purchased for less than $20,000. However, this price does not include the site for the home, which must be bought or leased separately.

Although mobile homes may not appreciate in value as rapidly as more traditional housing, depreciation can be minimized if the owner carefully selects the location and keeps the home in good repair.

The more expensive mobile or modular homes feature such conventional building items as shingle roofs and redwood siding. Inside, better mobile homes feature modern appliance-filled kitchens, fully equipped bathrooms and wall-to-wall carpeting. Mobile homes can have another advantage: they are fully furnished, so almost all a prospective owner needs besides financing and a toothbrush is food for the refrigerator and some plates to set the kitchen table.

Prices for mobile homes run about $13 per square foot of floor space, plus land. That's approximately fifty percent less than the average price of a stick-built home, which costs $25 to $30 a square foot, plus land.

Mobile homes are becoming so popular that they now account for nearly fifty percent of all new factory houses made. The line which separates a mobile home and a factory-built home is becoming finer all the time.

Technically, the mobile home has the wheels attached to its chassis. Modular and other factory houses, without wheels, are shipped on trucks. Once on the site, however, most mobile homes are permanently attached.

Although the local dealer may have only the wheeled versions on his lot, many mobile home manufacturers make both types of housing. They're turning out attractive modular houses, shipped in sections, that often cannot be distinguished by the inexperienced eye from the stick-built dwelling down the street.

Concern over mobile home construction need not worry the buyer. Today's mobile home is built according to the federal Mobile Home Construction and Safety Standards written by the Department of Housing and Urban Development (HUD). Every home built after June 15, 1976, must bear a seal indicating that it conforms to HUD standards. Enforcement of the federal standard also is the responsibility of HUD.

Prior to that date, forty-six states required compliance with the Mobile Home Standard as established by the National Fire Protection Association and the American National Standards Institute. The national code supersedes all state and local building codes to assure the consumer of a basically sound house. The code also makes both mobile homes and certain modular homes eligible for special Federal Housing Authority-insured home loans.

All financial institutions can lend to mobile home buyers. They are eligible for FHA or Veterans Administration (VA) loan insurance/guarantee programs. The Farmers Home Administration (FmHA) has authority to guarantee mobile home loans in rural areas.

Probably the most common method of retailer financing is through a chattel mortgage loan. The loan agreement originates through the sales agent or retailer, or is arranged by the home buyer directly with the financial institution. Like other forms of credit financing, mobile homes are subject to the "Truth in Lending" regulations. You must be told the annual percentage rate of interest you are being charged.

In areas of the country where double-wide and sectional homes are popular—especially when the land also is being purchased and financed—some institutions even offer extended

Nearly every piece in the pre-engineered house is cut at the factory, generally to size. All of this preplanning allows a number of pre-engineered homes to be completed two weeks or so after the parts shipment arrives at the site.

For most manufactured homes, the major components of the house interlock at the site, easing construction considerably. Wall planks, floor and roof decking often are tongued and grooved for easier assembly.
Photo courtesy of the American Plywood Association.

This house is actually two mobile units connected in the center patio area. Frequently, factory-built homes are bought through local dealer/builders who arrange for delivery and completion of the house, including modifications.

terms and set rates that resemble more closely the conventional mortgage associated with site-built housing.

Downpayments range from none at all under VA regulations to twenty-five percent or more under chattel mortgage plans. The most common down payment, though, is only ten percent. Loans may be obtained for up to twenty years, depending on the type of home and financing. Average maturities range from nine to eleven years.

Legislation is now pending in Congress that would extend the terms and raise the FHA loan ceilings. In the meantime, FHA- and VA-insured loans can be pooled and sold under the mortgage-backed securities program of the Government National Mortgage Association.

The VA mobile home loan guarantee was recently increased to fifty percent. In both FHA and VA programs, the mobile home must be built to the Mobile Home Construction and Safety Standards established by HUD in June, 1976.

Although the name implies they can be picked up and towed anywhere, mobile homes are not quite that flexible. Unlike the trailer homes of the past, many of today's models are quite large and need the assistance of professional movers.

One disadvantage is that mobile homes still are frowned upon by a number of city building department codes. Another disadvantage is that mobile home parks seldom offer long-term leases; the tenant may suddenly get hit with a massive rent jump.

Originally, all mobile homes were eight feet wide. Today they are available in fourteen-foot wide models and double-wide models, often twenty-four feet.

Probably the most common and economical mobile home is the single-wide unit—fourteen feet wide and seventy-three feet long. This style offers up to fourteen feet by sixty-nine feet of living space, or 966 square feet. The length of the towing hitch is customarily quoted in the overall dimensions of the home, but these three to four feet should not be included in the measurements for the actual living space.

Expandable mobile homes are made with additions that telescope inside the home during its highway movement, and then are placed into position at the homesite. Each section adds sixty to one hundred square feet of space to the room in which it is located. However, expandable models are becoming much less common and presently comprise less than two percent of the market.

Double-wides greatly increase the amount of living space. A typical model has twenty-four feet by sixty feet of living space, or 1,440 square feet. For double-wide units, two single units are built and towed separately to the site. On the site they are joined together to make one living unit. Double-wides must be carefully blocked and leveled so that roof leaks do not occur and heating ducts mesh properly. In some units, each section has its own furnace.

Prices for the different styles vary widely, based on local geographical construction requirements, the number of appliances, and the furnishings of the home. Local conditions and regulations also play a key role in the types and sizes of mobile homes offered in different parts of the country. Currently, forty-five states permit transportation of fourteen-foot wide mobile homes over highways. The five others still do not. In every mobile home area the local dealer should know the pertinent regulations and the necessary procedures for moving a home.

The Council of Better Business Bureaus recommends that you choose a mobile home retailer as carefully as you would select any type of home. The retailer may provide potential customers with the names and addresses of former customers. The retailer should also quote the overall cost of the home. The council suggests checking the local Better Business Bureau to find out if any complaints have been lodged against the firm.

The basic price of the mobile home generally includes a living room, a kitchen with range and

Kitchens have full size,
brand-name major appliances,
with the option of gas or electricity.
Photo: courtesy Manufactured
Housing Institute.

Factory-Built Housing— It's Come a Long Way

Generally, choosing a modular or factory built home allows the buyer to save about 15% as compared to the price of a conventional home.
Photo: Professional Builder

refrigerator, a dinette or separate dining room, one or two bathrooms, two or more bedrooms, cabinets and closets, an automatic heating system, a water heater, free-standing furniture, carpeting and other floor coverings, as well as curtains and draperies.

If a customer requests it, the retailer will sell a mobile home unfurnished. But this discount often will not make up for the cost of buying and adding the furniture yourself. The reason is simple: the manufacturer buys furnishings in quantity, so the allowance given will not equal the cost of the furnishings bought at retail prices.

Optional items that can be purchased as part of the home include central air conditioning, washer and dryer, dishwasher, garbage disposer, central vacuum-cleaning system and intercom system.

Quite often, the basic purchase price includes transportation of the mobile home to the site chosen by the buyer, as long as it is within a prescribed area set by the dealer. The dealer's personnel usually set up the mobile home for initial operation, but it's still wise to ask the dealer whether or not these items are included in the price. Of course, the sales contract should reflect these terms.

Most mobile homes are supplied with a combination of electrical and gas or oil appliances. Usually, the furnace is a warm-air system burning either gas or oil. The cooking range and water heater may use either gas or electricity. The refrigerator and dishwasher, if included, are electric.

In some of the more modern mobile home parks, a central system is used for distributing oil or gas to the individual homes. The type of gas appliances in the home must be matched to the type of gas available in the park. Where electric rates are low, mobile homes that are totally electric may be advantageous.

Besides the base price of the mobile home, you should count on paying for some on-site extras. A few are required by most parks. Industry authorities estimate these extras to add about fifteen percent to the cost of a mobile home. For instance, most parks require steps with handrails for every outside door. Concrete steps or runners or a base slab will have to be provided by the owner, unless the home is to be located in a park where sites are already prepared. Skirting, to conceal the wheels while still providing ventilation and access, and some form of supports or piers will probably also be required. They provide what is in effect a foundation, holding the home stable and level. Often concrete blocks are used.

Tie-down for protection against high winds must be provided by the mobile home manufacturer on all homes built in accordance with the national standard after January 1, 1974. Many states also require that mobile homes be anchored to the ground. While there are several types of anchors, the proper method of securing the home depends on its design as well as the site's soil and climatic conditions. Some lending institutions may require tie-down even if the home is not built in a park. Owners who have their homes anchored also may qualify for a lower insurance premium.

Optional extras that are frequently offered include garages, outdoor storage cabinets, cabanas, patios, awnings, porches and screened rooms. These are available from the retailer or a mobile home supply office.

The manufacturer or seller of a mobile home usually provides a warranty that guarantees the quality and workmanship of the home for a specified period of time. This warranty also tells the owner what to do if a problem arises.

Under a new federal warranty regulation that went into effect in 1975, warranties now must be designated by the manufacturer as "full warranty" (for the duration of the home) or "limited warranty." The manufacturers of both mobile and modular homes, as well as the makers of the appliances offered in the units, provide either a full or a limited warranty.

Factory-Built Housing— It's Come a Long Way

Careful buyers compare the terms of each. Be sure you recognize the difference between the manufacturer's and the retailer's responsibilities in setting up and servicing your home. Unless these are defined clearly at the time of the sale and put into writing, you could be headed for trouble.

Even if your mobile home and some of its appliances do not have written warranties, the buyer often has implied warranties under state laws. These laws generally require a mobile home and its appliances to work normally for a specified period of time.

Locating a mobile home on a private lot can be done, provided that local building codes are met. Check into this thoroughly before you take even preliminary steps. In some areas, permission is fairly easy to obtain for both mobile and modular housing. In other areas, both forms of housing are prohibited.

Start your search for a private lot by going to the local court house or city hall and obtaining a copy of the zoning ordinances applying to the area in which you are interested. Ask about receiving a variance in the zoning, should one be needed. If you are at all confused about the regulations, seek the advice of a local attorney. Whatever you do, do not buy a mobile or modular home before you know that you can meet all local requirements.

Don't forget the dealer, especially if he doesn't have a park of his own. He or she wants to sell you that home and may be able to give you valuable guidance about locating on private property.

Once you find a private site that suits you, there are some other items you should investigate. How far away are utilities to which you will need access? Will the local zoning ordinances allow you to add on to your home at a later date? How much will you need to pay in property taxes?

With these and other questions answered, you will have to hire a local contractor to prepare the site for your home. You will need either an approved foundation or properly prepared concrete strips or slab for the firm support of the home's piers. Local and state requirements may dictate the type of tie-down and anchorage the home will need.

You'll also need to investigate connections to electric, gas and telephone lines as well as to water and sewer mains, if available. In some parts of the country, the utilities companies insist that all connections be made by their own technicians. Even if they do not require you to use their staff, make sure that all connecting is done by qualified professionals.

If water and/or sewer hook-ups are not available near your building site, you may need to dig your own well and install your own septic system. Check local regulations concerning both.

Before you head for the drawing board, study the floor plans and designs of a number of manufacturers. If they don't offer you precisely what you want, at least they will provide you with a good head start in modifying the plans to suit your needs.

Appendix I:

State Chapters of the American Institute of Architects

Before you select an architect, you may wish to ask for some assistance from the local chapter of the American Institute of Architects. Most reputable architects are members of this association.

ALABAMA COUNCIL OF ARCHITECTS
P.O. Box 237
Montgomery 36101

ALASKA CHAPTER
505 W. Northern Lights
Anchorage 99503

ARIZONA SOCIETY
1109 North Second Street
Phoenix 85002

ARKANSAS CHAPTER
P.O. Box 2233
Little Rock 72203

CALIFORNIA COUNCIL
1736 Stockton Street
San Francisco 94133

COLORADO SOCIETY
1426 Larimer Street
Denver 80202

CONNECTICUT SOCIETY
85 Willow Street
New Haven 06511

DELAWARE SOCIETY
P.O. Box 157
Montchanin 19710

WASHINGTON D.C.
METROPOLITAN AREA
1777 Circle Street, N.W.
Washington 20036

FLORIDA ASSOCIATION
7100 North Kendall Drive
Suite 203
Miami 33156

GEORGIA ASSOCIATION
2525 Peachtree Center Building
230 Peachtree Street, N.W.
Atlanta 30303

HAWAII CHAPTER
1192 Fort Street Mall
Honolulu 96813

IDAHO CHAPTER
842 La Cassia Drive
Boise 83705

ILLINOIS COUNCIL
1800 South Prairie Avenue
Chicago 60616

INDIANA SOCIETY
1403 North Delaware Street
Indianpolis 46202

IOWA CHAPTER
621 Savings and Loan
Des Moines 50309

KANSAS CHAPTER
Merchants Tower
Suite 911
Topeka 66612

KENTUCKY CHAPTER
512 East Main Street
Lexington 40508

LOUISIANA CHAPTER
1925 Riverside North
Baton Rouge 70802

MAINE CHAPTER
One Middle Street
Hallowell 04347

MARYLAND SOCIETY
131 Main Street
Annapolis 21401

BOSTON SOCIETY
320 Newbury Street
Boston 02115

MICHIGAN SOCIETY
28 West Adams Street
Detroit 48225

MINNESOTA SOCIETY
Northwestern Bank Building
Suite 100
St. Paul 55101

MISSISSIPPI CHAPTER
P.O. Box 4661
Jackson 39216

MISSOURI COUNCIL
221 Madison Street
Jefferson City 65101

MONTANA CHAPTER
P.O. Box 503
Helena 59601

NEBRASKA CHAPTER
205 Executive Building
Omaha 68102

NEVADA CHAPTER
575 Forest Street
Reno 89502

NEW HAMPSHIRE CHAPTER
253 Myrtle Street
Manchester 03104

NEW JERSEY SOCIETY
110 Halsted Street
East Orange 07015

NEW MEXICO SOCIETY
3313 Girard
Albuquerque 87106

NEW YORK STATE ASSOCIATION
Three Northern Blvd.
Albany 12210

NORTH CAROLINA CHAPTER
The AIA Tower
15 West Morgan Street
Raleigh 27601

NORTH DAKOTA CHAPTER
269 Seventh Street North
Bismarck 58501

OHIO SOCIETY
37 West Braod
Suite 425
Columbus 43215

OKLAHOMA COUNCIL
101 Park Avenue Building
Suite 1313
Oklahoma City 73102

OREGON COUNCIL
200 Dakum Building
Portland 97204

PENNSYLVANIA SOCIETY
P.O. Box N
Harrisburg 17108

RHODE ISLAND CHAPTER
74 The Arcade
Providence 02903

SOUTH CAROLINA CHAPTER
P.O. Box 6101
Columbia 29260

SOUTH DAKOTA CHAPTER
118 South Main
Sioux Falls 57102

TENNESSEE SOCIETY
517 Union Street
Nashville 37219

TEXAS SOCIETY
800 Perry Brooks Building
Austin 78701

UTAH SOCIETY
555 East South Temple
Salt Lake City 84601

VERMONT CHAPTER
R.F.D. No. 1
Box 47
Waitfield 05673

VIRGINIA SOCIETY
15 South Fifth Street
Richmond 23219

WASHINGTON STATE COUNCIL
311 1/2 Occidental Avenue South
Seattle 98104

WEST VIRGINIA SOCIETY
P.O. Box 813
Charleston 25323

WISCONSIN CHAPTER
788 North Jefferson Street
Milwaukee 53202

WYOMING CHAPTER
P. O. Box FF
Jackson 83001

Appendix II:

National Association of Home Builders Chapters

There are many other chapters; one of them may be in your home town. However, by contacting the state or regional chapter, you can receive the name and address of the chapter nearest your home.

ALABAMA
1660 Montgomery Highway
Birmingham, 35216

ALASKA
750 E. Firewood
Anchorage, 99503

ARIZONA
5818 North 7th Street
Phoenix, 85014

ARKANSAS
Drawer R
Smackover, 71762

CALIFORNIA
400 S. El Camino Real #300
San Mateo, 94402

170 Newport Ct. Dr., St. #225
Newport Beach, 92660

COLORADO
P. O. Box 2008
Grand Junction, 81501

3835 W. 10th
Greeley, 80561

CONNECTICUT
27 Belltown Rd.
Stamford, 06905

74 W. Main St.
Norwich, 06360

DELAWARE
1035 Philadelphia Pike
Wilmington, 19809

Rural Route 6, Box 300
Dover, 19901

WASHINGTON, D.C.
P. O. Box 4346
Silver Spring, Md 20904

FLORIDA
P. O. Box 16561
Jacksonville 32216

9300 S. Dadeland Blvd #702
Miami, 33156

14483 62nd St. No.
Clearwater, 33520

1213 Densmore Dr
Winter Park 32792

P. O. Box 8026
Pensacola 32505

GEORGIA
5430 Jimmy Carter Blvd.
Norcross, 30093

HAWAII
3015 A Koapaka St.
Honolulu 96819

IDAHO
3613 Gekler Lane
Boise, 83706

Rt. 4 Box 157
Coeur D'Alene, 83814

P. O. Box 1641
Idaho Falls, 83401

ILLINOIS
31 Concord Drive
Oak Brook, 60521

10 E. College Drive
Arlington Heights, 60004

R. R. #1
Thompsonville, 62890

P. O. Box 1260
East St. Louis, 62207

INDIANA
801 W. Glen Park Ave.
Griffith, 46319

Rt. #3
Batesville, 47240

P. O. Box 45
Mexico, 46958

P. O. Box 153
Dyer, 46311

501 Bentbrook Dr.
New Albany 47150

IOWA
P. O. Box 114
Ankeny 50021

1743 N.W. 99th Court
Des Moines 50332

1102 Lake St.
Spirit Lake, 51360

KENTUCKY
P.O. Box 52
Florence, 41052

P.O. Box 43232
Louisville, 40243

Sunrise Drive
Madisonville, 42431

LOUISIANA
9204 Rhett Circle
Shreveport, 71108

MAINE
P.O. Box 168
Dover Foxcroft, 04426

MARYLAND
3708 Cardiff Ct.
Chevy Chase, 20015

MASSACHUSETTS
49 Cliffwood St.
Lenox, 01240

45 Albermarle Rd.
Norwood, 02062

89 Yarmouth Rd.
Hyannis, 02601

MICHIGAN
3279 Post Oak Drive
Clinton, 49236

3510 Pheasant Run Circle
Ann Arbor 48104

P.O. Box 21
Waters, 49797

MINNESOTA
8200 Humboldt Ave. So.
Bloomington 55431

R.R. 1
Sauk Rapids, 56379

2001 Brookdale Dr.
Minneapolis 55444

MISSISSIPPI
1115 Pass Road
Gulfport, 39501

P.O. Box 2338
Laurel 39440

MISSOURI
Box 1034
Columbia 65201

11426 Dorsett Road
Maryland Heights 63043

MONTANA
Star Route 138
Clancy, 59634

P.O. Box 945
Great Falls, 59401

725 Ronan
Missoula, 59801

NEBRASKA
3815 Touzalin Avenue
Lincoln, 68507

2404 Gateway Avenue
Grand Island, 68801

NEVADA
3355 Spring Mountain Rd.   3
Las Vegas, 89102

P.O. Box 1161
Carson City, 89701

NEW HAMPSHIRE
Hillside Terrace
Merrimack, 03054

11 Wedgewood Dr.
Londonderry 03053

NEW JERSEY
P.O. Box 399
Basking Ridge 07920

P.O. Box 387
Marlton, 08053

128 Cleveland Ave.
Colonia, 07067

127 Summit Ave.
Hackensack, 07601

NEW MEXICO
665 W. Main St.
Farmington, 87401

P.O. Box 5617
Santa Fe, 87501

NEW YORK
4029 St. Paul Blvd.
Rochester, 14617

992 South End
Woodmere, 11598

122 E. 42nd St.
New York, 10017

NORTH CAROLINA
P.O. Box 33608
Raleigh 27606

P.O. Box 6175
Asheville 28806

NORTH DAKOTA
Box 841
Minot, 58601

Box 1542
Grand Forks 58201

OHIO
812 Arbor Road
Circleville, 43113

P.O. Box 1798
Chillicothe 45601

OKLAHOMA
4113 Stratford Lane
Norman 73069

5600 N.W. 83rd St.
Oklahoma City, 73132

OREGON
9185 S.W. Oleson Rd.
Tigard, 97223

15300 S.W. 116th Ave.
Tigard, 97223

PENNSYLVANIA
P.O. Box 327
Fleetwood, 19522

1401 Jamie Dr.
Monroeville, 15146

P.O. Box 2392
Bellefonte, 16823

PUERTO RICO
Centro Comm. Unicoop   205
Rio Piedras, 00926

RHODE ISLAND
177 Old River Road
Lincoln, 02865

SOUTH CAROLINA
746 St. Andrews Blvd.
Charleston, 29407

SOUTH DAKOTA
301 Mt. Rushmore Rd.
Rapid City, 57701

700 West 43rd
Sioux Falls 57105

TENNESSEE
Two Int'l Plaza,   600
Nashville, 37217

P.O. Box 38080
Memphis 38138

TEXAS
6415 San Felipe
Houston 77057

4740 Millcreek Rd.
Dallas 75234

3201 81st St.
Lubbock 79413

UTAH
P.O. Box 1045
Orem, 84057

5906 Lakeside Drive
Salt Lake City, 84121

VIRGINIA
8204 Westmeath Lane
Richmond, 23227

P.O. Box 1259
Lynchburg, 24505

1301 Beverly Rd.
McLean, 22101

WASHINGTON
16107 N.E. 33rd Ave.
Ridgefield, 98642

2100–112th N.E.
Bellevue, 98004

WEST VIRGINIA
1211 Pineview Dr.
Morgantown, 26505

4498 Country Club Blvd.
So. Charleston, 25309

5th Ave.
Ranson, 25414

WISCONSIN
917 S. Randall Avenue
Janesville, 53545

R.R. 6
Chippewa Falls 54729

Box 495
Woodruff, 54568

WYOMING
P.O. Box 1904
Rock Springs, 82901

1214 E. 21st
Cheyenne 82001

1558 Hyview
Casper, 82601

200 West Hogeye
Gillette, 82716

Appendix III:

National Home Improvement Council, Inc.

11 East 44th Street
New York, New York 10017

The National Home Improvement Council chapters are located in the following areas:

BIRMINGHAM, ALA.

BOSTON, MASS.

BUFFALO, N.Y.

CANTON (STARK COUNTY), OHIO

CHATTANOOGA, TENN.

CHICAGO, ILL.

CINCINNATI, OHIO

CLEVELAND, OHIO

COLUMBIA, S.C.

DALLAS, TEXAS

DENVER, COLO.

DETROIT, MICH.

ERIE, PENN.

GRAND RAPIDS (WESTERN), MICH.

HOUSTON (SOUTH TEXAS), TEX.

KANSAS CITY, MO.

LITTLE ROCK, ARK.

MILWAUKEE, WIS.

LONG ISLAND, N.Y.

PITTSBURGH (WESTERN), PENN.

PORTLAND, ORE.

ST. LOUIS, MO.

SALT LAKE CITY, UTAH

SEATTLE, WASH.

SPRINGFIELD, (WESTERN), MASS.

WASHINGTON, D.C.

Appendix IV:
American Building Contractors Association

2476 Overland Avenue
Los Angeles, Ca 90064

The following chapters of the American Building Contractors Association are affiliated with NHIC:

COACHELLA VALLEY, CALIF.

LOS ANGELES, CALIF.

NORTH TAHOE, CALIF.

ORANGE COUNTY, CALIF.

SACRAMENTO, CALIF.

SAN DIEGO, CALIF.

SAN FRANCISCO (BAY AREA), CALIF.

TULARE-KINGS COUNTY, CALIF.

Appendix V:
Dome Home Manufacturers and Builders

Those marked with an asterisk belong to the recently-established National Association of Dome Home Manufacturers. There may be others in your locale. However, before you sign anything, the author recommends checking out any dome manufacturer as thoroughly as you research your architect and contractor. If you have an architect or contractor already, ask him or her to look over the plans in-depth before agreeing to buy. Remember, few legitimate businesses will mind having their references checked. In fact, many welcome such careful inspection. You may also wish to write the National Association of Dome Home Manufacturers, 1701 Lake Avenue, Suite 470, Glenview, Illinois 60025

ALABAMA

Dr. Milton Norrell
1716 First Avenue, North
Pell City 35125

R. E. Vance
Route 3, Box 498A
Pell City 35125

ALASKA

Cathedralite Domes
SRA Box 1561-Z
Anchorage 99507

ARIZONA

21st Century Living
Route 1, Box 218
Saint David 85630

Dyna-Dome
22226 North 23rd Avenue
Phoenix 85027

Synergetics
P.O. Box 1112
Parker 85344

ARKANSAS

Ozark Domes
P.O. Box 268
Fayetteville 72701

CALIFORNIA

Cathedralite Domes
P.O. Box 886
Aptos 95003

Dome West
181 Pier Avenue
Santa Monica 90405

Domeplans
P.O. Box 2351
La Mesa 92041

*Envirotecture
134 North Ojai Street
St. Santa Pamla 93060

Free Space Geodescis
7094 North Harrison
Suite 165
Pinedale 93650

Monterey Domes
3777-B Placentia Avenue
Riverside 92507

TEMCOR
2825 Toledo Street
Torrance 90503

The Polydome Company
1238 Broadway
El Cajon 92021

Timberline Geodesics
2015 1/2 Blake Street
Berkeley 94704

COLORADO

Earth Dynamics, Inc.
P.O. Box 1175
Boulder 80302

Geodesic Domes
Manufacturing & Sales
P.O. Box 1675
Bailey 80421

Tecton Corporation
P.O. Box 0
Boulder 80306

FLORIDA

Key House
1450 Madruga Avenue
Coral Gables 33146

Yaca-Dome, Inc.
Route 5, Box 409
Lake Placid 33852

IDAHO

Vandenbark Geometric
Construction, Inc.
P.O. Box 907
Kimberly 83341

ILLINOIS

*American Dome Builders
142 Hillcrest Avenue
Wood Dale 60191

*Tom Borman Company
6544 Tennessee Avenue
Clarendon Hills 60514

*Creative Dome Company
942-1 Volbrecht Road
Crete 60417

*Domes America, Inc.
6 S 771 Western Avenue
Clarendon Hills 60514

*Solar Domes, Inc.
321 West Northwest Highway
Barrington 60010

IOWA

*Domiciles, Inc.
Route 1
Numa 52575

New Age Builder, Inc.
704 East Adama
Fairfield 52556

*Smith Productions, Ltd.
R.R. 4, Box 122A
Cherokee 51012

MAINE

American Geodesic, Inc.
Kennebec Road, Box 164
Hampden Highlands 04445

Domaine
P.O. Box 55
Mount Desert 04660

Domescape
P.O. Box 458
Hyannisport 02647

*Hasey Company
447 North Main Street
Old Town 04468

MARYLAND

Dome Designs, Inc.
12468 Lime Kiln Road
Fulton 20759

The Domes Company
736 22nd Street, NW
Washington, D.C. 20052

Geodesic Builders, Inc.
P.O. Box 7
Monkton 21111

MASSACHUSETTS

Allard Enginering
South Lee 01260

MICHIGAN

Geodesic Manufacturing
10290 Davison Road
Davison 48423

Tension Structures, Inc.
9800 Ann Arbor Road
Plymouth 48170

MINNESOTA

*The Big Outdoors People, Inc.
2201 North East Kennedy Street
Minneapolis 55413

Hexadome of Minnesota
R.R. 2, Box 106A
Mankato 56001

MONTANA

Big Sky Dome Structures
390 Third Avenue, West North
Kalispell 59901

NEVADA

Argi-Dome
420 East Park, No. 3
Carson City 89701

Desert Domes
5508 West Lake Mead Blvd.
Las Vegas 89108

NEW JERSEY

*Domes & Homes, Inc.
P.O. Box 365
Brielle 08730

NEW MEXICO

Creative Structures, Inc.
P.O. Box 143
Alto 88312

Zomeworks Corporation
P.O. Box 712
Albuquerque 87103

NEW YORK

Dome East Corporation
325 Duffy Avenue
Hicksville 11801

EGGE Research
Box 59H RFD 1
Catskill 12414

Fuller & Sadao
32-37 Vernon Blvd.
Long Island City 11106

Geodesic Dome
Manufacting Company
P.O. Box 602
Plattsburgh 12901

OHIO

Geodesic Enclosure Systems, Inc.
1007 South High Street
Columbus 43206

TEXAS

Texas Geodesics, Inc.
Route 1, Box 127C
Bedford 76021

Western Hemisphere, Ltd.
8113 Rush Street
Fort Worth 76116

VIRGINIA

Semispheres
P.O. Box 26273
Richmond 23260

WISCONSIN

*Amherst Domes, Inc.
P.O. Box 248
Amherst 54406

Dome Home Systems, Inc.
Route 2, Box 247A
Reedsburg 53959

*Domes/Geodyssey Corporation
P.O. Box 206
Amherst 54406

*Kettle Moraine Domes
1134 Greenway Lane
P.O. Box 955
West Bend 53095

WYOMING

Synaps, Inc.
P.O. Box 90
Route 62
Lander 82520

Appendix VI:

Log Home Manufacturers

Here's a list of some of the log home manufacturers, alphabetized by state for easy reference. If you are seriously considering this alternative you may wish to contact a number of the companies. Many have dealer/builders across the country.

COLORADO LOG HOMES
1925 W. Dartmouth
Englewood, Co. 80033

BUILDING LOGS, INC.
P.O. Box 300
Gunnison, Co. 81230

NATIONAL BEAUTI-LOG CEDAR HOMES
1250 South Wilson Way
Stockton, Ga. 95205

LODGE LOGS BY MACGREGOR
3200 Gowen Road
Boise, Idaho 83705

YOUNGSTROM LOG HOMES
Box 385
Blackfoot, Idaho 83221

NORTHERN PRODUCTS, INC.
Bomarc Road
Bangor, Me. 04401

NORTHEASTERN LOG HOMES
Kenduskeag, Me. 04450

L. C. ANDREW, INC.
28 Depot Street
South Windham, Me. 04082

WARD CABIN COMPANY
P.O. Box 72
Houlton, Me. 04730

BELLAIRE LOG CABIN MFG.
P.O. Box 322
Bellaire, Mich. 49615

HERITAGE LOG HOMES
3739 South Lindbergh
St. Louis, Mo. 63127

OZARK LOG HOMES
Highway 86
Eagle Rock, Mo. 65641

ROCKY MOUNTAIN LOG HOMES
Box 1255
Hamilton, Montana 59840

MODEL LOG-LBR ENT INC.
Star Route, Box 203
Bozeman, Montana 59715

NATIONAL LOG CONSTRUCTION CO.
P.O. Box 68
Thompson Falls, Montana 59873

ROCKY MOUNTAIN LOG HOMES
Box 1255
Hamilton, Montana 59840

CHISUM INDUSTRIES INC.
110 N. Cleburn Box 1966
Grand Island, Neb. 68801

PIONEER LOG HOMES
P.O. Box 267
Newport, N.H. 03773

CROCKETT LOG HOMES INC.
Route 9
W. Chesterfield, N.H. 03466

LOK-N-LOGS INC.
Rt. 80, RD 2, Box 212
Sherburne, N.Y. 13460

ALTA INDUSTRIES LTD.
P.O. Box 88
Halcottsville, N.Y.

R & L LOG BUILDING INC.
R.D. #1
Guilford, N.Y. 13780

RAYSTOWN LAND COMPANY
RD #1
James Creek, Pa. 16657

NORTHERN COUNTRIES
Rt. 50 West, Box 97
Upperville, Va. 22176

GREEN MOUNTAIN CABINS
Box 190
Chester, Vt. 05143

VERMONT LOG BUILDINGS
Hartland, Vt. 05048

RUSTIC LOG STRUCTURES
14000 Interurban Ave. S.
Seattle, Wa. 98168

SYLVAN PRODUCTS INC.
4729 State Hwy 3, S.W.
Port Orchard, Wa. 98366

PAN ABODE CEDAR HOMES
4350 Lake Washington Blvd.
Renton, Wa. 98055

JUSTUS COMPANY INC.
P.O. Box 91515
Tacoma, Wa. 98491

WILDERNESS LOG HOMES
Route 2
Plymouth, Wis. 53073

AUTHENTIC HOMES
P.O. Box 1288
Laramie, Wy. 82070

CANADA

CALGARY SASH & DOOR LTD.
735-41 Avenue N.E.
Calgary, Alberta T2E3P9

CEE-DER-LOG BUILDING LTD.
1215 McKnight Blvd. N.E.
Calgary, Alberta T2E 5T1

CLASSIC LOG LTD.
Box 333
Lac LiBiche, Alberta TOA 2CO

NEW DAWN HOUSING LTD.
Box 998
Lac LaBiche, Alberta TOA 2 CO

TRUNOR LOG IND (1976)
Farmington
D.C., Canada VOC 1NO

TRUE CRAFT LOG STRUCTURE
60 Riverside Drive
North Vancouver, B.C. V7H1T4

PAN ABODE BUILDING LTD.
20900 Westminster Hwy
Richmond, B.C. V6V 1V5

FINN LOG MANUFACTURING
1490 Gaulais Ave. N.
Salt Ste Marie
Ontario, Canada

HOMESTEAD LOGS LTD.
7027 Yonge St.
Thronhill, Ontario L3T 2A5

INTERNATIONAL LOG HOMES
Box 129
Mill Bay, B.C. VOR 2PO

LAURENTIAN LOG HOMES
36 Rt. 117, Box 219
Val Morin, Quebec JOT 2RO

CAN AM LOG HOUSE LTD.
P.O. Box 1297
Waterloo, QUEBEC JOE 2NO

Appendix VII:

Mobile, Modular Manufacturers

Many of the companies listed offer potential customers both modular and mobile housing alternatives. You may discover others in your area. This listing is broken down by state and will get you started. Although you may wish to start with companies in your own area, don't restrict your search since many companies can supply you with their product lines through a distributor in your area.

ALABAMA

ADDISON INDUSTRIES, INC.
Eagle Homes Division
P.O. Box 169
Addison, 35540

THE COMMODORE CORPORATION
P.O. Box 520
Haleyville, 35565

FESTIVAL HOMES OF ALABAMA, INC.
100 Fleetwood Drive
P.O. Box 628
Reform, 35481

FRANKLIN HOMES INC.
Route 3
Russellville, 35653

GUERDON INDUSTRIES, INC.
P.O. Box 312
Alexander City, 35010

HOLIDAY HOMES INC.
P.O. Box 157
Lynn, 35595

FAIRWAY HOMES
P.O. Box 550
Hamilton 35570

PENTHOUSE INDUSTRIES INC.
P.O. Drawer H
Phil Campbell 35581

REDMAN HOMES INC.
P.O. Box 459
Boaz 35957

WINSTON INDUSTRIES, INC.
P.O. Box 347
Double Springs, 35553

MARIETTA HOMES
P.O. Box 346
Double Springs 35553

CRIMSON HOMES
P.O. Box 407
Double Springs 35553

SHILOH HOMES
P.O. Box 497
Double Springs 35553

SUNSHINE HOMES INC.
P.O. Box 507
Red Bay 35582

TIDWELL INDUSTRIES, INC.
P.O. Box 679
Haleyville 35565

DOLPHIN HOMES
P.O. Box 820
Haleyville 35565

MARION HOMES
P.O. Drawer 101
Bear Creek 35543

TIDWELL HOUSING SYSTEMS INTERNATIONAL
P.O. Box 679
Haleyville 35565

ARIZONA

FLEETWOOD ENTERPRISES, INC.
Fleetwood Homes of Arizona Inc.
738 VIP Avenue, P.O. Box 577
Casa Grande 85222

FUQUA HOMES INC.
802 South 59th Street
Phoenix 85009

KAUFMAN & BROAD HOME SYSTEMS
5530 W. Bethany Home Road
Glendale 85301

MODULINE INDUSTRIES INTERNATIONAL
MODULINE INDUSTRIES (ARIZONA) INC.
P.O. Box 248
Chandler 85224

NATIONAL MOBILE HOMES
309 So. Perry Lane
Tempe 85281

REDMAN HOMES INC.
P.O. Box 626
Chandler 85224

SCHULT HOMES CORPORATION
P.O. Box 908
Buckeye 85326

ARKANSAS

GUERDON INDUSTRIES, INC.
P.O. Box Drawer B-2
Beebe 72012

GUERDON INDUSTRIES, INC.
P.O. Box Drawer N
Cabot 74222

GUERDON INDUSTRIES, INC.
P.O. Box 369
Manila 72422

GUERDON INDUSTRIES, INC.
P.O. Box 4132
North Little Rock 72116

CALIFORNIA

BARON HOMES INC.
P.O. Box 805
13821 Redwood Avenue
Chino 91710

BENDIX HOME SYSTEMS INC.
2245 West Valley Blvd.
Colton 92324

BENDIX HOME SYSTEMS INC.
13538 Excelsior Drive
Santa Fe Springs 90670

BENDIX HOME SYSTEMS, INC.
P.O. Box 1427
11 N. County Road 101
Woodland 95695

CALIFORNIA DESIGN HOMES INC.
1621 E. 17th St., Suite S
Santa Ana 92701

CHAMPION HOME BUILDERS CO.
P.O. Box 429
Lindsay 93247

CONCORD HOMES DIVISION
P.O. Box 964
Dinuba 93618

DMH COMPANY
620 North Iowa, P.O. Box 1185
Redlands 92373

DUALWIDE HOMES
601 East Wooley Road
Oxnard 93030

FASHION MANUFACTURED HOMES INC.
22135 Alessandro Street
Riverside 92508

FLEETWOOD ENTERPRISES INC.
P.O. Box 7638
3125 Myers Street
Riverside 92503

DIVISIONS:

BARRINGTON HOMES INC.
6001 20th St., P.O. Box 3529
Rubidoux 92509

FESTIVAL HOMES INC.
797 El Mira Road, P.O. Box 790
Vacaville 96588

FLEETWOOD HOMES INC.
7007 Jurupa Ave., P.O. Box 4038
Riverside 92504

FLEETWOOD HOMES OF NORTHERN
CALIF.
18 N. County Rd. 101, P.O. Box 1308
Woodland 95695

SANDPOINTE MOBILE HOMES INC.
1600 Clancy St.
Visalia 93277

SUNCREST HOMES INC.
27126 Watson Rd., P.O. Box 878
Perris 92370

FUQUA HOMES INC.
14286 East Sixth Street
Corona 91720

FUQUA HOMES INC.
P.O. Box 909
Marysville 95901

GUERDON INDUSTRIES, INC.
P.O. Box 330
Woodland 95695

GUERDON INDUSTRIES, INC.
21243 Ventura Blvd., Suite 137
Woodland Hills 91364

HERITAGE INDUSTRIES
375 So. Cactus Ave., P.O. Box 854
Rialto 92376

KAUFMAN & BROAD HOME SYSTEMS INC.
1081 National Boulevard
Los Angeles 90064

DIVISION:

11320 Amalgam
Rancho Cordova 95670

KIT MANUFACTURING COMPANY
1700 Santa Fe Avenue
Long Beach 90813

L.C.S. HOMES INC.
10800 Kalama River Road
Fountain Valley 92708

MODULE INTERNATIONAL INC.
Module Industries (Calif) Inc.
P.O. Box 2185
Manteca 95336

PACIFIC LIVING SYSTEMS
15670 Perris Blvd.
Sunnymead 92388

PEPSICO BLDG. SYSTEMS INC.
3031 La Jolla Street
Anaheim 92806

PEPSICO BLDG. SYSTEMS INC.
9550 Turner Avenue
Cucamonga 91730

REDMOND HOMES INC.
22201 Alessandro Blvd.
Riverside 95208

REDMIC INDUSTRIES INC.
P.O. Box 826
Chino 91710

SHELTER RESOURCES CORPORATION
Lancer Homes Inc. Div.
1660 Old Magnolia
Corona 91720

SILVERCREST INDUSTRIES INC.
8700 Stanton Avenue
Buena Park 90620

STURGIS MOBILE HOMES INC.
17061 Compton Avenue
Corona 91720

SUN VALLEY HOMES INC.
11182 Penrose St.
Sun Valley 91352

CANADA

FLEETWOOD HOMES OF ALBERTA, INC.
4050 77th Street, P.O. Box 800
Red Deer, Alberta

MARLETTE HOMES OF CANADA LTD.
703 Dooro Street
Stratford, Ontario

MODULE INDUSTRIES (MARITIMES) LTD.
P.O. Box 425
Amherst, N.W., Canada B4H 325

MODULE INDUSTRIES (QUEBEC) LTD.
P.O. Box 700
Drujmondville, Quebec J2B 6W6

MODULINE INDUSTRIES (CANADA) LTD.
P.O. Box 190
Penticton, British Columbia V2A 6K3

MODULE INDUSTRIES (ALBERTA) LTD.
P.O. Box 5000
Red Deer, Alberta T4N 5L6

COLORADO

CHAMPION HOME BUILDERS
Titan Homes Division
P.O. Box 10
Berthoud 80513

GUERDON INDUSTRIES
P.O. Box 811
Longmont 80501

REDMAN HOMES INC.
3842 Redman Drive
Ft. Collins 80521

FLORIDA

BENDIX HOME SYSTEMS INC.
2415 Griffin Road
Leesburg 32748

CELTIC CORPORATION
1930 Tampa E. Blvd.
Tampa 33619

CHAMPION HOME BUILDERS CO.
Manatee Homes Division
P.O. Box 1238
Oneco 33558

CONCORD HOMES DIVISION
P.O. Box 119
Lake City 32055

FLEETWOOD ENTERPRISES INC.
Barrington Homes of Florida Inc.
1603 Grove Ave., P.O. Box 37
Haines City 33844

FLEETWOOD ENTERPRISES INC.
Glenbrook Homes of Fla. Inc.
4848 Sydney Airport Rd., P.O. Drawer PP
Plant City 33566

FLEETWOOD ENTERPRISES INC.
Suncrest Homes of Florida
2433 A2 Park Road, Drawer F
Lakeland 33802

FUQUA HOMES INC.
P.O. Box 608
Auburndale 33823

GUERDON INDUSTRIES INC.
P.O. Box 1847
Lake City 32055

GUERDON INDUSTRIES INC.
P.O. Box 1207
Belleview 32620

HOUSING BY VOGUE INC.
P.O. Box 2253
Tallahassee 32304

HOUSING BY VOGUE INC.
P.O. Box 303
Lake City 32055

LIBERTY HOMES INC.
495 Oak Road
Ocala 32670

NATIONAL MOBILE HOMES
P.O. Box 1117
Dunedin 33528

PEPSICO BLDG. SYSTEMS INC.
605 South Frontage Road
Plant City 33566

REDMAN HOMES INC.
P.O. Box G
Eaton Park 33840

SCHULT HOMES CORPORATION
P.O. Box 4038
Sarasota 33580

VINDALE CORPORATION
642 Mabry Street
P.O. Box 2477
Tallahassee 32304

ZIMMER HOMES CORPORATION
777 S.W. 12th Avenue
Pompano Beach 33061

GEORGIA

DeROSE INDUSTRIES INC.
P.O. Box 1076
Bainbridge 31717

THE FAIR-MOORE CORPORATION
P.O. Box 800
Thomasville 31792

FLEETWOOD INDUSTRIES INC.
Fleetwood Homes of Georgia Inc.
Northside Industrial Park
P.O. Box 272
Douglas 31533

GUERDON INDUSTRIES, INC.
P.O. Box 1081
Waycross 31501

GUERDON INDUSTRIES INC.
P.O. Box 1356
Waycross 31501

GUERDON INDUSTRIES INC.
P.O. Box 1449
Waycross 31501

HOUSING BY VOGUE INC.
Housing By Tiffany Div.
P.O. Box 1080
Moutrie 31768

LIBERTY HOMES INC.
Industrial Blvd., P.O. Box 145
Thomasville 31792

MARLETTE HOMES INC.
Americus 31709

MIDLAND INDUSTRIES INC.
Cullip Industries Div.
P.O. Box 386
Ellaville 31806

NATIONAL MOBILE HOMES
Warrenton Highway
P.O. Box 955
Thomson 30824

REDMAN HOMES INC.
P.O. Box 319, Hwy 280E.
Richland 31825

C. O. SMITH INDUSTRIES INC.
P.O. Box 490
Moultrie 31768

C. O. SMITH INDUSTRIES INC.
Peachtree Housing
Pavo Road
Moultrie 31768

C. O. SMITH INDUSTRIES INC.
Tall Oaks Homes Div.
Moultrie 31768

VINTAGE HOMES INC.
3825 N.E. Expressway
Atlanta 30340

VINTAGE HOMES INC.
P.O. Box 1478
Gainesville 30501

GEORGIA

ARABI HOMES INC.
P.O. Box 117
Arabi 31712

BENDIX HOME SYSTEMS INC.
61 Perimeter Park
Atlanta 30341

BENDIX HOME SYSTEMS INC.
1051 Old Lindale Road
Rome 30161

BRIGADIER INDUSTRIES CORP.
P.O. Box 954
Thomson 30824

CHAMPION HOME BUILDERS CO.
Mobile Home Division
P.O. Box 5
Ellaville 31806

DMH COMPANY
Eaton Hwy, 411 North
Milledgeville 31061

DARLINGTON ENTERPRISES
Box Y
Tifton 31794

DEEP SOUTH MOBILE HOMES
OF GEORGIA
P.O. Box 8
Person 31642

IDAHO

CHAMPION HOME BLDRS.
Sequoia Homes Div.
P.O. Box 70
Weiser 83672

CHAMPION HOME BLDRS.
Tamarack Homes Division
P.O. Box 190
Weiser 83672

CHAMPION HOME BUILDERS
Concord Homes Division
P.O. Box 525
New Plymouth 83655

CHAMPION HOME BUILDERS
Titan Homes Division
P.O. Box 188
Parma 83660

CONCHEMCO CORPORATION
200 N. Maple Grove Road
Boise 83705

CONCHEMCO CORPORATION
Drawer S, Hwy 68 E. of City
Mountain Home 83647

FLEETWOOD ENTERPRISES INC.
Broadmore Homes of Idaho Inc.
2611 E. Comstock, P.O. Box Drawer L
Nampa 83651

FLEETWOOD ENTERPRISES INC.
112 Industrial Road
Nampa 83651

GUERDON INDUSTRIES INC.
Box 5188, Whitney Station
Boise 83705

KAUFMAN & BROAD HOME
SYSTEMS INC.
5500 Federal Way
Boise 83705

KIT MANUFACTURING COMPANY
P.O. Box 250
Airport Ave., & Warehouse Rd.
Caldwell 83605

ILLNOIS

APECO CORPORATION
Homebuilders Group
2100 Dempster Street
Evanston 60204

NATIONAL MOBILE HOMES
P.O. Box 319
Anna 62906

INDIANA

ADMIRATION HOMES INC.
51788 State Road No. 19
Elkhart 46514

ALL AMERICAN HOMES, INC.
P.O. Box 451
309 South 13th Street
Decatur 46733

BENDIX HOME SYSTEMS, INC.
South Elm Rd. & Country Rd. 128
Bourbon, 46504

C & G CORPORATION
29449 U.S. 33 West
P.O. Box 218
Elkhart 46514

BARON MOBILE HOMES
29449 U.S. 33 West
P.O. Box 218
Elkhart 46514

RAINBOW CORPORATION
29449 U.S. 33 West
Elkhart 46514

COAHMEN HOMES CORPORATION
P.O. Box 705
Middlebury 46540

COACHMEN INDUSTRIES, INC.
P.O. Box 30
Middlebury 46540

CROYDON HOMES CORPORATION
P.O. Box 610
Middlebury 46540

DE ROSE INDUSTRIES INC.
4002 Meadows Drive
Suite 116
Indianpolis 46205

DON A BELL HOMES INC.
P.O. Box 11
54635 CR 17S
Elkhart 46514

ELCONA HOMES CORPORATION
P.O. Box 520
2200 Middlebury Street
Elkhart 46514

MEMORY HOMES
P.O. Box 1042
Elkhart 46514

FAIRMONT HOMES, INC.
P.O. Box 27
County Road No. 7
Nappanee 46550

FESTIVAL HOMES OF INDIANA
100 Festival Drive
P.O. Box 344
Brazil 47834

FLYNN INDUSTRIES INC.
1201 Markley Road
Plymouth 46563

GLOBEMASTER MOBILE HOMES INC.
P.O. Box 206
Goshen 46526

SWIFT MOBILE HOMES
2901 Oakland
P.O. Box 848
Elkhart 46514

HIGHLAND HOMES INC.
P.O. Box 158
Swayzee 46986

LIBERTY HOMES INC.
1101 Eisenhower Dr. No.
P.O. Box 35
Goshen 46526

LIBERTY HOMES INC.
P.O. Box 608
Syracuse 46567

MANUFACTURED HOMES INC.
29089 Lexington Park Dr.
Elkhart 46514

MANUFACTURED HOMES INC.
28936 Phillips St., P.O. Box 272
Elkhart 46514

MANUFACTURED HOMES INC.
Certified Homes Div.
1100 North Woodlawn
Elkhart 46514

MANUFACTURED HOMES INC.
Spring Manor Homes Div.
29269 Lexington Park Dr.
Elkhart 46514

MONARCH INDUSTRIES INC.
P.O. Box 1
Goshen 46526

DIVISIONS:

CAMBRIDGE HOMES DIVISION
P.O. Box 176
Syracuse 46567

COPPES KITCHENS
Nappanee, 46650

FAWN DIVISION
P.O. Box 125
Syracuse 46567

MONARCH HOMES
P.O. Box 125
Syracuse 46567

REGENT HOMES
P.O. Box 176
Syracuse 46567

NATIONAL MOBILE HOMES
P.O. Box 680
Lafayette 47902

NEW YORKER HOMES
701 Collins Road
Elkhart 46514

PARKWOOD HOMES INC.
P.O. Box 237
Elkhart 46514

PATRIOT HOMES INC.
51420 C.R. 3 South
Elkhart 46514

REDMOND HOMES INC.
P.O. Box 95
Topeka 46571

REDY-KWIK HOMES INC.
2914 Clifty Drive
Madison 47250

RITZ-CRAFT HOMES
401 S. West
Argos 46501

ROCHESTER HOMES INC.
P.O. Box 587
East Lucas Street
Rochester 46975

SCHULT HOMES CORPORATION
P.O. Box 151
Middlebury 46540

SKYLINE CORPORATION
2520 By-Pass Road
Elkhart 46514

TIDWELL INDUSTRIES INC.
Bristol Homes
P.O. Box 591
Goshen 46526

TORCH INDUSTRIES INC.
2701 Mishawaka Road
P.O. Box 685
Elkhart 46514

U.S. INDUSTRIES INC.
Gerring Industries Inc. Div.
R.R. No. 1, P.O. Box 1-B
Shipshewana 46565

VEMCO BUILDERS INC.
P.O. Box 1012, County Rd. No. 15
Pine Creek Industrial Park
Elkhart 46514

VICTORIAN HOMES INC.
P.O. Box 707
County Road N. 14
Middlebury 46540

ZIMMER HOMES CORPORATION
Duke Mobile Homes Div.
Kesco Drive
Bristol 46507

Richmond Homes Inc. Div.
P.O. Box 336
Richmond 47374

Windsor Mobile Homes Inc. Div.
P.O. Box 337
Bristol 46507

INDONESIA

P. T. ASA ENGRG. PERTAMA
J1. Panglima Polim Raya 15-c
Kebayoran Baru, Jakarta
Jakarta Selatan
Indonesia

KANSAS

BENDIX HOME SYSTEMS INC.
1550 Davis St.
Ottawa 60067

CHIEF INDUSTRIES INC.
Bellavista Homes
P.O. Box 553
Russell 67665

CONCHEMCO INC.
Homes Group
P.O. Box 2078
Shawnee Mission 66201

DMH COMPANY
P.O. Box 388, Meridian Rd.
Newton 61114

DMH COMPANY
400 So. Halstead St.
Hutchinson 67501

FLEETWOOD ENTERPRISES
Broadmore Homes of Kansas Inc.
1220 Hatcher St., P.O. Box 868
Emporia 66801

GUERDON INDUSTRIES INC.
P.O. Box 1106
Manhattan 66502

KIT MANUFACTURING COMPANY
P.O. Box 738, One Kit Blvd.
McPherson 67460

LIBERTY HOMES INC.
P.O. Box 18
Yoder 67585

MARLETTE HOMES INC.
Great Bend 67530

SCHULT HOMES INC.
P.O. Box 409
Plainville 67663

KENTUCKY

CAROLINA INTERNATIONAL INC.
1 Hurstbourne Park
9200 Shelbyville Road
Louisville 40222

GUERDON INDUSTRIES INC.
P.O. Box 35290
Louisville 40232

SCHULT HOMES CORP.
P.O. Box 397
Guthrie 42234

LOUISIANA
FUQUA HOMES INC.
P.O. Box 883
Ruston 71270

HOLIDAY HOMES INC.
P.O. Box 997
Mansfield 71052

SHELTER RESOURCES CORP.
Sherwood Homes Division
P.O. Box 2156
Natchitoches 71456

MARYLAND
SCHULT HOMES CORP.
P.O. Box 21921

MICHIGAN
CHAMPION HOME BUILDERS CO.
5573 E. North St.
Dryden 48428

DMH COMPANY
Div. National Gypsum Co.
1517 Virginia St.
St. Louis 48880

MOBILELIFE CORPORATION DIV.
1517 Virginia St.
St. Louis 48880

DEROSE INDUSTRIES INC.
P.O. Box 97
Cassapolis 49031

LOG MARK HOMES
Travelo Homes Co.
P.O. Box 1427
Saginaw 48605

MARLETTE HOMES INC.
3270 Wilson St.
Marlette 48453

SQUIRE HOMES INC.
P.O. Box 98
Constantine 49402

STERLING CORPORATION
P.O. Box 415
White Pigeon 49099

MINNESOTA
BENDIX HOME SYSTEMS INC.
P.O. Box 190
Worthington 56187

CHAMPION HOME BUILDERS INC.
Titan Homes Division
P.O. Box 89
Slayton 56172

DMH COMPANY
100 Third Street
Red Lake Falls 56750

DEROSE INDUSTRIES INC.
P.O. Box 586
Owatonna 55060

MODULE INTERNATIONAL INC.
Moduline (Minn.) Inc.
P.O. Box 147
Montevideo 56265

SCHULT HOMES CORP.
P.O. Box 399
Redwood Falls 56283

U.S. INDUSTRIES INC.
Gerring Industries
P.O. Box 446
Blue Earth 50013

MISSISSIPPI
BENDIX HOME SYSTEMS INC.
Int'l Site, Old Airport Road
Brookhaven 39601

FLEETWOOD ENTERPRISES
FLEETWOOD HOMES OF MISS. INC.
100 Fleetwood Circle P.O. Box 0
Lexington 39095

GUERDON INDUSTRIES INC.
P.O. Box 230
Vicksburg 39180

GUERDON INDUSTRIES INC.
P.O. Box 271
Eupora 39744

TIDWELL INDUSTRIES INC.
LaSalle/Madrid Homes
P.O. Box 518
Ripley 38663

VINTAGE HOMES INC.
P.O. Box 38
Clarksdale 38641

MISSOURI
FUQUA HOMES INC.
P.O. Box 354
Boonville 65233

SHELTER RESOURCES CORP.
Sun Dancer Homes Div.
P.O. Box 308
Noel 64854

NEBRASKA
CHAMPION HOME BUILDERS CO.
P.O. Box 189
York 68467

CHAMPION HOME BUILDERS CO.
P.O. Box 148
Central City 68826

CHIEF INDUSTRIES INC.
Housing Division
P.O. Box 349
Aurora 68818

CHIEF INDUSTRIES INC.
Bonnavilla Homes Div.
P.O. Box 127
Aurora 68818

GUERDON INDUSTRIES INC.
P.O. Box 588
Gering 69341

REDMAN HOMES INC.
1515 E. Fourth St.
Grand Island 68801

WESTERN HOMES CORP.
P.O. Box B
North Bend 68649

NEW YORK
CHAMPION HOME BUILDERS CO.
P.O. Box 56
Sangerfield 13455

CHAMPION HOME BUILDERS CO.
P.O. Box D
Richfield Springs 13439

FLEETWOOD ENTERPRISES INC.
Festival Homes of N.Y. Inc.
Cadyhill Industrial Park
P.O. Box 371
Saratoga Springs 12866

SHELTER RESOURCES CORP.
Schoonmaker Homes Inc.
Temple Hill Road, Box 98
Vails Gate 12584

VINDALE CORPORATION
P.O. Box V, Powers Rd.
Conklin 13748

NORTH CAROLINA

CAROLINA INTERNATIONAL INC.
Carolina Homes
P.O. Box 488
Rockwell 28138

CHAMPION HOME BLDRS CO.
Mobile Home Division
P.O. Box 1146
Lillington 27546

TITAN HOMES DIVISION
P.O. Box 11385
Lillington 27546

CONCHEMCO INC.
P.O. Box 709
Siler City 27344

CONNER HOMES CORPORATION
P.O. Box 520
Newport 28570

FLEETWOOD ENTERPRISES INC.
Broadmore Homes of N. C. Inc.
P.O. Box 665, Hwy 87 at Hwy 29
Reidsville 27320

FESTIVAL HOMES OF N.C. INC. DIV.
County Rd. 1774, P.O. Box Drawer 99
Marshville 28103

FUQUA HOMES INC.
P.O. Box 1208
Henderson 27536

HAVELOCK HOMES CORP.
P.O. Box 249
Havelock 28532

HOUSING BY VOGUE INC.
P.O. Box 1116
Pembroke 28372

MANSION HOMES CORPORATION
P.O. Box 756
Robbins 27325

OAKWOOD HOMES CORPORATION
P.O. Box 7385
Greensboro 27407

REDMAN HOMES INC.
P.O. Box 2686
Hwy 421 & Cox Mill Rd.
Sanford 27330

REDMAN HOMES INC.
Hwy 70 East, Rt. 1
P.O. Box 340
Mebane 27302

SCHULT HOMES CORPORATION
P.O. Box 127
Polkton 28135

R-ANELL HOMES INC.
P.O. Box 236, Hwy 16
Denver 28037

C. O. SMITH INDUSTRIES INC.
Peachtree Housing
Oxford 27565

TIDWELL INDUSTRIES INC.
Tidwell of North Carolina
Route 1, Box 208T
Rockwell 28138

VISCOUNT MFG. CO.
P.O. Box 337
Rockwell 28138

OHIO

BARRINGTON HOMES OF OHIO
1032 S. Maple St., P.O. Box 108
Bowling Green 43402

FLEETWOOD ENTERPRISES
FESTIVAL HOMES OF OHIO
P.O. Box 98, 40 Seminary St.
Greenwich 44837

FUQUA HOMES INC.
P.O. Box 308
Caldwell 43724

MIDLAND INDUSTRIES INC.
111 E. 4th Street
Cincinnati 45202

MOBILE HOME ESTATES INC.
R.R. 4
Bryan 43506

SHELTER RESOURCES CORPORATION
The Office Place
24200 Chagrin Blvd.
Beachwood 44122

UNBILT INDUSTRIES INC.
P.O. Box 373
Vandalia 45377

VINDALE CORPORATION
630 Hay Avenue
Brookville 45309

VINDALE CORPORATION
600 Albert Road
Brookeville 45309

OKLAHOMA

REDMAN HOMES INC.
12539 Skelly Drive
Tulsa 74128

OREGON

BENDIX HOME SYSTEMS INC.
1801 Orchard Avenue
McMinnville 97128

THE COMMODORE CORPORATION
P.O. Box 578
Lebanon 97355

FLEETWOOD ENTERPRISES INC.
Sandpointe Homes of Oregon Inc.
2555 Progress Way, P.O. Box 156
Woodburn 97091

FUQUA HOMES INC.
P.O. Box 1227
Bend 97701

GUERDON INDUSTRIES INC.
P.O. Box 370
Stayton 97383

KIT MANUFACTURING CO.
P.O. Box 365
2238 Yew Street
Forest Grove

LIBERTY HOMES INC.
P.O. Box 188
Sheridan 97378

MARLETTE HOMES INC.
Hermistan 97838

MODULE INTERNATIONAL INC.
Module Industries Inc.
P.O. Box 168
Aumsville 97325

REDMAN HOMES INC.
1204 Mill St.
Silverton 97381

PENNSYLVANIA

APECO CORPORATION
Newport News
Route 443
Pine Grove 17963

BENDIX HOME SYSTEMS INC.
P.O. Box 349
Clarion 16214

CHAMPION HOME BUILDERS CO.
Atlantic Homes Div.
P.O. Box 256
Claysburg 16625

CONCHEMCO INC.
304 Streibeigh
Montoursville 17754

DMH COMPANY
P.O. Box 350
Clarion 16214

DEROSE INDUSTRIES INC.
P.O. Box Drawer K
Chambersburg 17201

FLEETWOOD ENTERPRISES INC.
Broadmore Homes of Pa. Inc.
100 Fleetwood Dr., P.O. Box 300
Ringtown 17967

LIBERTY HOMES INC.
21 So. Groffdale Rd., P.O. Box 129
Leola 17540

MARLETTE HOMES INC.
Lewistown 17044

POLORON HOMES OF PA.
74 Ridge Road
Middleburg 17842

REDMAN HOMES INC.
P.O. Box 428
Ephrata 17522

ZIMMER HOMES CORP.
PENNSYLVANIA DIV.
West Sassafras St.
Selingsgrove 17870

SOUTH CAROLINA

GARDENIA HOMES INC.
Box 211
Laurens 29360

MASCOT HOMES INC.
P.O. Box 127
Gramling 29348

SOUTH DAKOTA

U.S. INDUSTRIES INC.
4733 N. Cliff Avenue
Sioux Falls 57104

GUERDON INDUSTRIES INC.
P.O. Box 26
Madison 57042

TENNESSEE

APECO CORPORATION
Townhouse Inc.
P.O. Box 449
Selmer 38375

CHAMPION HOME BUILDERS CO.
Atlantic Homes Division
P.O. Box 3507
Henry 38231

CONCHEMCO INC.
P.O. Box 86
Greenfield 38230

FLEETWOOD ENTERPRISES INC.
Glenbrook Homes of Tenn. Inc.
Fleetwood Drive at Hawkins St.
P.O. Box 600
Westmoreland 37186

MOBILE HOME ESTATES INC.
Modular Structures Div.
Tiny Town Road, P.O. Box 2296
Clarksville 37040

NORRIS INDUSTRIES INC.
Highway 11-W
Bean Station 37708

VINDALE CORPORATION
Crossland Homes Inc.
216 Davis St.
Crossville 38555

TEXAS

APECO CORPORATION
Craftmade Homes Div.
P.O. Box 1185
Henderson 75652

BENDIX HOME SYSTEMS INC.
P.O. Box 5517
Texarkana 75501

CAROLINA INTERNATIONAL INC.
Carolina Homes of Texas
P.O. Box 1684
Lufkin 75901

CELTIC CORPORATION
7001 Imperial Drive
Waco 76710

CHAMPION HOME BUILDERS CO.
Manatee Homes Div.
P.O. Box 663
Commerce 75428

MOBILE HOME DIVISION
P.O. Box 459
Buffalo 75831

METAMORA HOMES DIV.
P.O. Box 260
Wills Point 75169

TITAN HOMES DIV.
P.O. Box 185
Honey Grove 75446

CHIEF INDUSTRIES INC.
Bonnavilla Homes
P.O. Box 509
Gainesville 76240

CONCHEMCO INC.
2400 Burkburnett Rd.
Wichita Falls 76307

DEROSE INDUSTRIES INC.
P.O. Drawer C
Bonham 75418

FLEETWOOD ENTERPRISES INC.
Broadmore Homes of Texas Inc.
2800 E. Industrial Rd., P.O. Box 370
Waco 76703

FLEETWOOD ENTERPRISES INC.
2801 Gholson Rd., P.O. Box 149
Waco 76705

Sandpointe Mobile Homes of
Texas Inc.
Como St., P.O. Box 816
Sulphur Springs 95482

FUQUA HOMES INC.
7100 So. Cooper
Arlington 76015

KAUFMAN & BROAD HOME SYSTEMS
INC.
Wayside Homes Div.
600 E. Watauga
Saginaw 76079

NATIONAL MOBILE HOMES
6935 Ryan Drive
Austin 78757

PERM-A-DWELL CORP.
P.O. Box 417
McGregor 76657

REDMAN HOMES INC.
Redman Plaza East
2550 Walnut Hill Lane
Dallas 75229

REDMAN HOMES INC. DIVISIONS:

P.O. Box 1330
Hwy 31W
Athens 75751

501 S. Burleson Blvd.
Bulreson 76028

2126 Marshall Drive
Grand Rapids 75061

SCHULT HOMES CORP.
P.O. Box 571
Navasota 77868

U.S. INDUSTRIES INC.
1000 Expressway Tower
Dallas 75206

VINTAGE HOMES INC.
P.O. Box 632
Breckenridge 76024

UTAH

CHAMPION HOME BUILDERS CO.
P.O. Box 638
Brigham City 84302

VIRGINIA

CHAMPION HOME BUILDERS CO.
Concord Homes Division
P.O. Box 465
Mt. Jackson 22842

THE COMMODORE CORPORATION
P.O. Box 300
Danville, 24541

THE COMMODORE CORPORATION
P.O. Box 300
Danville 24550

FLEETWOOD ENTERPRISES INC.
Fleetwood Homes of Virgina
Hwy 40 West, RFD 4, P.O. Box 100
Rocky Mount 24151

UNITIZED SYSTEMS CO. INC.
718 E. Atlantic St.
P.O. Box 127
South Hill 23970

WASHINGTON

BARRINTON HOMES OF WASHINGTON
111 S. Pekin Rd., P.O. Box 250
Woodland 98674

FLEETWOOD ENTERPRISES INC.
Fleetwood Homes of Washington Inc.
2925 Index Road, P.O. Box 165
Washougal 98671

MODULE INTERNATIONAL INC.
Executive Offices
P.O. Box 209
Chelais, 98532

MODULINE INTERNATIONAL INC.
Moduline Industries Inc.
P.O. Box 1106
Chelais 98532

WISCONSIN

DICKMAN HOMES INC.
Box 378
Spencer 54479

FLEETWOOD ENTERPRISES INC.
Fleetwood Homes of Wisconsin Inc.
2400 W. Wisconsin Service Rd.
P.O. Box 443
Portage 53901

LIBERTY HOMES INC.
P.O. Box 338
Dorchester 54425

ROLLOHOME CORPORATION
115 E. Upham
Marshfield 54449

Index